RAISING A GROWNUP

Parenting Tweens, Teens, and
Twenty-somethings into Thriving,
Successful, Independent Adults

Erick Lauber, Ph.D.
with Riley Yonchiuk
and Haley Brown

Leadership Media

Copyright © 2024 Erick Lauber

All rights reserved

No part of this book may be reproduced, or stored in a retrieval system, or transmitted in any form or by any means, electronic, mechanical, photocopying, recording, or otherwise, without express written permission of the publisher.

ISBN: 978-0-9883829-5-4 (print)
ISBN: 978-0-9883829-6-1 (e-book)

CONTENTS

Title Page
Copyright
Preface
Chapter 1 - The Roadmap to Successful, Happy Adults   1
Chapter 2 - The Parenting Backstory   11
Chapter 3 - How to Guide Your Young Adult   25
Chapter 4 - Raising a Healthy Adult   42
Chapter 5 - Social Wellbeing and Navigating Relationships   72
Chapter 6 - Finding and Engaging with Your Community   93
Chapter 7 - Finding a Career You Love and Value   111
Chapter 8 - Financial Wellbeing Isn't All About Money   132
Epilogue   153

PREFACE

As a cognitive psychologist and college faculty for over 30 years - and as a co-parent of three wonderfully complex young adults, now aged 30, 29 and 27 - I've advised and navigated the tumultuous seas of parenting through the tween, teen, and twenty-something years. I've experienced firsthand the frustration of unanswered texts, the worry over new friendships, and the challenge of discussing life's big questions. It's these personal and professional experiences that motivated me to write this book. After creating the GrowingUpSucksPodcast.com for college students and the DecodingTodaysYouth.com parenting blog, it became apparent to me that much more needed to be said about raising thriving, successful, happy young adults - but most importantly, independent young adults who can take care of themselves. COVID surely added to the anxiety of our current young adults. It also contributed to their lack of grit and life skills. I see that everyday in the college environment. So, what are we going to do about it?

I think we need to step back and realize our job as parents is not to protect our children for the rest of their lives, but to grow in them the confidence and decision-making skills they need to take care of themselves. In this book I break that task down. First, I diagnose "wellbeing" into five categories backed by internationally-recognized research by the Gallup organization.

This research helps me answer the question, "What does a thriving and successful adult life look like?" Then I work backward to ask, "OK, so how do we get there?" The answer is "Raising a Grownup". In this book I hope to provide practical guidance on what you can be doing right now to help your children thrive later in life. I call this the WISE ADULT approach. Let me know what you think about it.

Before we begin, I have to thank the many students who have helped me with all of my projects over the years. Most recently that includes the two teams that worked on the blog and the podcast, but this project was pushed over the finish line by two outstanding young women, Riley Yonchiuk and Haley Brown. Haley has graduated but was the constant sounding board through out the outlining stage of this book. She also helped at the writing stage and was a wonderful help with her English degree and honest feedback. Riley jumped in more recently but was the driving force and really kept me on track. She provided a reality check on everything we discussed and has great writing skills herself. I could not have written this without their patience, insights, and, most importantly their perspective and stories - which you'll find scattered throughout the book.

I'd also like to thank my family for giving me permission for writing this book. We were not and still are not perfect parents. It takes quite a lot of courage to throw yourself out there as an "expert" in such a personalized endeavor. Who knows what feedback we'll get when we tell our true, authentic stories. But my family understood I felt this was necessary. If we can help anyone raise healthier, happier, more successful young adults with high wellbeing, it would be worth it. Thank you Betsy, Casey, Emily, and Jesse, and my own parents and siblings.

Whether you're in the thick of parenting tweens, teens or twenty-somethings, or just approaching these critical years, "Raising a Grownup" is designed to enlighten, guide, and transform your family life. Let's get going.

Erick Lauber
Erick Lauber, Ph.D., is an applied psychologist and faculty at Indiana University of Pensylvania. Currently he teaches leadership, AI, interactive media, and journalism courses. His research is on community health and wellness, and his scholarship has appeared in more than 100 magazines and books. His educational media products have also won over two dozen national awards including the Telly Awards and the Broadcast Educator Association.. His most recent parenting articles have appeared in Parent News, Apple Family Works, Women's Sourcebook, Today's Family Now, and Positively ADHD. Recently his students helped him produce the parenting blog DecodingTodaysYouth.com which resulted in the book Your Kid's World Today. His team also produced the college-targeted podcast, GrowingUpSucksPodcast.com.

Erick and his wife, Betsy, live in Indiana, Pennsylvania, hometown of Jimmy Stewart. They've been married 33+ years and their three kids have all moved out. They are enjoying being "empty nesters", though Erick still misses having the kids around sometimes. Casey, 30 (boy), lives in Pittsburgh; Emily, 29 (girl), lives in Seattle; and Jesse, 27 (boy), lives in Colorado Springs, CO.

Riley Yonchiuk
Riley Yonchiuk is a 20-year-old from Harrisburg, Pennsylvania. She is currently a sophomore at Indiana University of Pennsylvania and is majoring in Communications Media in the News Media track and minoring in Art Studio. She is a DJ at IUP's radio station, WIUP-FM. Riley also serves as the Traffic Director for the station, and works to promote campus and community organizations and events across WIUP's programming schedule.

In her free time, she enjoys staying busy and active. Riley

finds joy in creating art, painting and practicing her craft with different Adobe programs, such as Adobe Illustrator and Adobe Photoshop. She is also fond of running, working out, and being outdoors. Growing up with her two brothers and parents in a sports loving household, she hopes to one day work in sports broadcasting or athletic communications.

Haley Brown
Haley Brown is a 25-year-old from Gilbertsville, Pennsylvania. She graduated from Indiana University of Pennsylvania in 2022 with degrees in English Writing, and Ecology and Conservation Biology. She currently enjoys work at a garden center as a social media and marketing manager. She also acts as a buyer for the garden center's annuals and houseplant departments and is a self-proclaimed Jack-of-all-trades around the garden center.

When not working, she often finds herself at the garden center anyway, adding to her personal houseplant collection and her own garden beds. She loves spending time outdoors, being active, reading, writing, editing, and spending time with her cat, Tino. She hopes one day to find a remote writing job that gives her plenty of flexibility and freedom to travel and see the world, since she's spent much of her life in her small town of Gilbertsville.

CHAPTER 1 - THE ROADMAP TO SUCCESSFUL, HAPPY ADULTS

An Erick Story: The Night The Police Called

"It was after midnight when the phone rang next to my wife's side of the bed. I'm slow to wake up, so it took a few tries before she made it clear, 'This one is yours.' The policeman explained with great patience over the phone that I needed to come pick up my son. He'd been arrested outside a college house party and would not be allowed to drive our car home.

When I arrived four blocks from campus, the police lights lit up the quiet street. A couple of other parents were picking up their high schoolers and my son was sitting in the car we let him drive. The policeman explained the kids had been breathalyzed and all of them had been drinking. My son got out of the car and tried to apologize to the officer again, but I was getting angry and embarrassed and told him to go sit in my car. As we drove home, I found out he had had one can of beer called a 'Four Loco'. I later learned this beer held the caffeine equivalent of 6 cups of coffee and the alcohol content of 4-6 cans of beer. (They've since changed the formula.) I watched my son get more drunk as time passed. I am grateful the police stopped him from driving.

Earlier that night, my son had told us he was going to a bonfire at *another high schooler's house. He had never mentioned he was going to pick up a bunch of kids and go to a college party. We'd been lied to. That incident taught us that even a good kid, a popular kid, a pretty smart kid, could make a terrible, dangerous decision. We learned you can trust your kid most of the time, but probably not all of the time.*

We re-learned how to drive our 16-year-old back and forth to school every day, while he spent three months being grounded. His friends were allowed over to the house, but he couldn't go out because we didn't believe he would be honest about where he was going. We learned he was the only one of the kids from that night who were grounded or were made to do community service.

Once he was allowed out again, we bought a breathalyzer and administered it every time he went out. When we showed up in court, our son was rightfully terrified of what he might face. We learned we were the only ones who hadn't hired a lawyer. There was a fine involved and he was responsible for paying for it out of his savings. After the court visit we walked across the street to the bank and as my son was making the withdrawal from his account, the teller who knew our son asked if he was buying a present for someone. He admitted to the teller he was paying a court fine and she looked him straight in the eye and said, 'You won't do that again, will you?' I remember him saying 'No, Mrs E.' About a year or two later, the penalty was expunged from his record. In the meantime, he learned that any future run-ins with the law would have much more severe consequences.

This book is not about bragging about how well my wife and I did everything. We didn't. And we don't have perfect kids. But then again, no one does. Probably no one ever will. We got through that major life episode and had plenty more to get through. But I want you to know that you can get through even the most upsetting and disappointing events. Our son, so far, has never had another run-in with the law. He graduated college with honors, found his calling in the business world, and is now doing well. Our worst fears have not come to pass. Hopefully, yours won't either. To up the chances your kid will be able to take care of themself, I wrote this book. Parenting is certainly a tough job. But, it is the toughest job you'll ever love."

Instead of starting at the typical "once upon a time," we're going to flip the script and begin at the "happily ever after." Let's envision the end goal. What do we want our kids to become when they grow up? The common answer might be "happy," but let's dig deeper. Parenting successfully is not about crafting everlasting happiness for them – that's chasing rainbows. Parenting our kids well is about fostering independence and responsibility, empowering them to be captains of their own happiness. In the language of modern psychology, we're aiming for "thriving" kids. Trying to make them happy forever is not the right goal.

Depending on your kids' ages and your relationship with them, you might wonder about your influence on this journey. Can you really steer them towards thriving adulthood? The answer is a resounding and enthusiastic "yes". With my background in cognitive psychology and my wife's expertise in developmental psychology, we've witnessed the growth of responsible, independent young adults who are thriving. They are not without their headaches and heartaches, of course, and we still get the occasional stressed out phone call. We're all human, after all. But overall, I'd have to say they are doing just fine, and, importantly, they are able to take care of themselves. We've talked out a few major life decisions with them in recent years, but we certainly don't lean in to any particular choice. We let them make their choices.

If I could summarize this whole book into one sentence it would be: "you want your child to one day parent themselves." What I mean by that is that you want them to take the initiative and begin guiding themselves toward future successes with the tools you raised them to use. When you can answer "yes" to the question: "Can they take care of not just their present self, but their future self as well?", you've done your job.

But we need to break down this concept of "thriving". It's more than a buzzword; it's a new take on the pursuit of wellbeing. A couple decades ago, researchers in positive psychology began exploring what it means to live a fulfilling life. What does a "good life" look like? What is the proper definition of "thriving"? Being successful? How do we have high "wellbeing"? The researchers analyzed the results, wrote great summaries, and published a best-selling book: "Wellbeing: The Five Essential Elements" by Tom Rath and Jim Harter (2010).

In Rath and Harter's research, conducted through the Gallup organization, hundreds of thousands were surveyed (and Gallup still does this research). The answers were separated into the five following key areas: physical and emotional health, social connections, community engagement, career satisfaction, and financial stability. According to this research, excelling in these domains is the secret to thriving. I wholeheartedly endorse this way of looking at a happy, thriving life. In my own experience, making sure we are taking care of ourselves in these five areas is the best place to start at making our lives as fulfilling and as happy as we can. I've also had the good fortune of being a professor to thousands of young adults, and taught or coached hundreds of teenagers. I'm also a part-time leadership instructor and have coached many mid-career adults in work-life balance and communication skills. Since my discovery of Rath and Harter's book I've used these five categories endlessly to focus peoples' time, talent, and treasure toward the things that really matter. When you're done with "Raising a Grownup" I think you'll agree. If we can get anyone, including ourselves, to take care of their own lives in these five areas, they are going to be in great shape.

In this book, we'll explore each of these categories, offering practical advice to set your children up for success in these areas. If they can master being independent, responsible, empathetic, and satisfied in each of these categories, they'll be well on their way to becoming a successful adult.

The Goldilocks of Parenting: Strict, Lenient, or Just Right?

Before we dive into the five categories, let's address parenting styles. You may have heard about authoritarian, permissive, and authoritative parenting, as well as the debates over helicopter versus free-range parenting. We won't get too caught up in labels, but our approach resembles the authoritative parenting style, or what's now termed "free-range parenting". Let's explore these styles.

The distinctions between parenting styles often boils down to how parents balance discipline and communication/support. Authoritarian parents, for example, have high expectations and demands for their children, but are low on responsiveness. That means they are low on communication, warmth, and support. An authoritarian parenting style values obedience over independence. This can lead to rule-following children, but it may also lead to lower self-esteem and weaker social skills. And "woah" look out when they suddenly become rule-breaking children.

Permissive parents are lenient, highly nurturing, and communicative. They often act more like a friend than a parent. Sounds fun, but this dynamic can result in children struggling with self-discipline and lacking respect for authority. There is much more that could be said about these styles so feel free to research "parenting styles".

The "Goldilocks" style is "authoritative" (not "authoritarian") parenting, which balances high responsiveness with high demands. These parents are nurturing, yet set clear boundaries, promoting independence within defined limits. This approach often leads to children who are confident and socially aware.

You might have heard of two extreme styles of parenting that have recently gotten press. The first is called "neglectful parenting". It's characterized by both low demands and low responsiveness. They simply ignore their children. The opposite of neglectful parenting is "helicopter parenting". These parents intervene in their childrens' lives and attempt to exact control over them. They try to solve every problem and clearly don't raise independent children. This book is against overparenting. We're not training any helicopter pilots here.

"Free-range parenting" emphasizes independence and self-reliance, but within developmentally appropriate boundaries. This allows children to explore, take risks, and learn from their experiences, while remaining in a safe and guided environment. I'm going to advocate for this style because it nurtures self-sufficient adults. And, in case you've heard of him, at times this book might sound like a pretty famous parenting guru named John Rosemond. I think he would advocate for free-range parenting. If you enjoy this book, I recommend his work to you.

As we proceed, remember, parenting is not a one-size-fits-all journey. It's a complex balancing act, requiring adaptability, patience, self-awareness, and understanding. Our goal is to provide you with a roadmap, drawing from both research and personal experiences, to navigate this very important undertaking.

A Haley Story: Helicopter Parenting At Its Worst

"A former romantic partner of mine had an extremely strict, controlling, helicopter mother. His father was passive and never dared to disagree with her. My boyfriend was living with his parents rent-free, so he was more than willing to be a responsible member of the household. He did all the dishes, took the dogs out, and always looked after his siblings. However, his mother saw him as an inexhaustible resource and he felt powerless to correct this misgiving. She asked him constantly, with no notice, to forgo plans he'd made with me and his friends to pick up his siblings, asked him to fix things around the house at his own expense, and gave him endless grief when he wasn't at home. He would be in huge trouble when he got back if she didn't know where he'd been, or if he got home even a few minutes later than what he told her. Eventually, she decided she didn't like how much time he was spending with me. She claimed I was distracting him from his job and his family obligations. He and I had frequent fights about this topic.

'Why won't you stand up for us? Have you told her that you love me? That I want what's best for you, too? That I make you happy?'

In contrast, my mother and I have great communication. I feel I can always tell her when she's said something that crossed the line. I can set boundaries with her. I'm allowed to be an adult. So I had a lot of difficulty comprehending a parent-child relationship where there was zero communication coming from the child. I felt that his parents didn't care if he was happy. Having zero boundaries baffled me. Why wouldn't a parent want their kid to become a self-sufficient, happily independent adult?

He told me he didn't feel safe standing up for himself, disagreeing with his parents, or setting any kind of boundary with them. One night, he and I reached a pivotal point. We were sitting in my bedroom, finishing up the same difficult talk we'd had many-a-time about him needing to learn how to set boundaries with his folks. We sat in silence for a few minutes and then he looked at me with an apology already in his eyes. There was no hint of resistance or anger in his expression, so the words he said next took a few moments to register.

'My mom says I can't sleep over at your place anymore.' I stared at him, dumbfounded. A joke? Judging from the way he wouldn't meet my eyes, I knew it wasn't. All I could muster was: 'You're 22.' He shrugged helplessly, still unable to meet my eyes.

We fought about it for another three months. Finally, we gave up and called our relationship off. The situation wasn't going to change anytime soon, no matter how much we cared for one another, and we were both suffering because of the circumstances. He was stuck between a rock and a hard place and we had to choose what was best for us both.

I hope someday he is able to make space for himself and express his wants and needs to his parents. I hope desperately that they learn to start listening. Their extreme helicopter parenting has, even so far, been damaging to him and his siblings as well. I know it must be difficult to stand back and let your child do their thing. It'll probably be hard knowing they might not need you as much as they used to, but in the end, that's the goal of being a parent. Letting them take off on their own journey and hoping you've done a good enough job. If you do that and can build a strong enough relationship with them, I think they'll happily bring you along for the ride."

The Five Key Areas of Wellness

We'll explore each of the five key areas of wellness that we mentioned above in detail, providing insights and strategies to help you help your children not only grow, but excel in each category. From encouraging physical and emotional health to fostering strong social connections, from engaging in meaningful community activities to pursuing satisfying careers and managing finances wisely, we aim to cover all the important bases.

In each chapter, we'll share research findings and practical tips, all aimed at equipping you with the tools to guide your children toward adulthood. You will also be hearing anecdotes from myself and two fellow contributors. Riley, a young college student, and Haley, a college graduate, are both on their own journeys to becoming self-sufficient adults. We'll share our personal experiences and address common challenges. We'll offer solutions to help ensure that you're prepared for the various scenarios you might encounter along the way. Sometimes we'll tell the stories of our friends. Note, they don't all end with "and we did the right thing". We learn from our mistakes - including how to parent.

Remember that the ultimate goal is not just to raise successful children, but to nurture well-rounded adults. We're not just looking at the here and now; we're setting our sights on the future. This isn't a sprint; it's a marathon—a journey that will have its share of challenges and triumphs. What I can tell you as the current parent of a 30-, 29-, and 27-year-old, parenting is the toughest job you'll ever love.

To guide your young adult towards independence and success, you need to understand what thriving means. This isn't just about doing well in a career; it's about excelling in all aspects of life. My favorite definition of wellbeing comes from the previously mentioned research done by the Gallup organization. We will dedicate an entire chapter to exploring each of the five topics in greater detail. Let's look at each briefly.

Careers: Not Just Jobs, But Joy

Gallup's research brought to light an intriguing insight: the significant role one's career plays in shaping one's perception of a thriving life. Interestingly, it's not about the financial aspect of a career – finances are a different matter altogether. The focus is more on how we spend our time, particularly in enjoying our daily activities. A thriving career is about engaging in work that feels meaningful and purposeful. Can we find joy in our day-to-day tasks, which, for most of us, revolve around our jobs? You can guide your child to discover what they love to do within the context of their strengths. Aligning those strengths with a career path is crucial in setting them up for success. If they have a passion for graphic design, for example, securing an internship in that field can be invaluable. Finding work that challenges them, yet allows for creativity, can make their work experience exceptionally fulfilling.

Social Sphere: The Art of Relationships

Social wellbeing is about nurturing strong, loving relationships in your life. This concept extends beyond romantic connections; it encompasses cultivating a supportive network of family, friends, and colleagues. It's essential for all of us to have people to share our joys and triumphs with, and to feel supported and accepted by a community. As your young adult steps out of your home nest, it's important for them to find ways to continue making social connections on their own, while maintaining the close connections they've already formed.

Finance: More Than Numbers

We're all aware that money holds some importance in our lives. There's a mountain of knowledge to be acquired in managing finances effectively. The goal for your child in this realm is to have the ability to manage their economic life efficiently. It's about their understanding of how to spend wisely and live within their means. Financial wellbeing isn't synonymous with being wealthy; rather, it's about having financial security and the freedom to make choices. Ideally, you'd like to guide your young adult to establish a budget, responsibly handle their expenses, and even start setting aside a small portion of their income for future significant expenses. It's also wise to educate them on the prudent use of credit cards, and the importance of building a credit score before they step out independently.

Physical Wellbeing: Beyond the Gym
Physical wellbeing extends beyond mere strength or fitness; it's also about possessing the energy required for daily tasks. There's a direct correlation between one's quality of life and health. As many of us are aware, maintaining physical and emotional health involves engaging in regular physical activities, eating nutritiously, and ensuring adequate rest. Consider what you envision for your young adult as they grow up. Perhaps it's someone who jogs three times a week and participates in yoga, or someone adept at cooking balanced, nutritious meals. We'll discuss these aspirations and then work backwards, strategizing ways to encourage these goals.

Community: Feeling at Home
In the Gallup survey, participants also emphasized the importance of feeling connected to their community. This not only entails feeling safe and taking pride in their community, but also being actively engaged in their local area. You'd hope for your grown child to be involved in community activities, feeling that they are contributing positively to their world. It's understood that involvement, be it volunteering monthly at a local food bank, or participating in community clean-ups, fosters a deep sense of connection to the neighborhood.

This brief overview reveals the complexity and depth of these topics. Each one could be, and has been, the subject of entire books – I can attest to that, having read them. However, our approach here is to refine the key points, striving to extract the most useful and practical advice. This wisdom will equip us, as parents, with the tools we need to raise children who are not only successful and thriving, but also independent.

CHAPTER 2 - THE PARENTING BACKSTORY

If you're already a parent you know what this job entails. Constant responsibility. Never ending "crises". And an extremely steep, never-ending learning curve. Being a parent is a tough job. But it's not like it's never been done before. In fact, unless you were raised by wolves, you've seen somebody already do the job. Hopefully you think successfully.

But we don't have to parent like our parents. Nor like anyone else on our block. But we should lay out how different this job is from nearly every other job. First, let's compare it to one job that might seem close - coaching.

The Parenting and Coaching Comparison

Have you ever heard that being a parent is a bit like being a coach? I've coached all my kids in different sports and activities, and you know, there's some truth to it. There are definitely a few tricks from the coaching playbook that come in handy when you're a parent. But, let's be real. Parenting and coaching aren't exactly the same game.

When we think about how parenting is like coaching, most folks think of the big-time sports like basketball or football. But if we're looking for a coaching style that parallels parenting, I'd say a track coach is a more accurate comparison. As the resident expert for an entire high school track team, you have to be knowledgeable about a wide range of skills, just like parenting.

There's also the lack of recognition. Unlike the "big sports", track coaches just like parents often work behind the scenes without much fame or acknowledgment. Plus, everyone seems to have advice on how you could do things better. There is alway someone right outside the fence yelling their coaching instructions to you or your child. Also, there are times when the kids may not appreciate the effort and discipline you are instilling in them. Just like coaching track. But, hey, it's all part of the job, right? At least most of the time you get to parent indoors.

Parenting as Coaching

The coaching-parenting comparison can go further. Especially in less obvious ways. Neither role is always about actively teaching skills. Sometimes, it's about the intangible things that aren't really related to acquiring knowledge or skill. Think about the end of track season when all the kids head off for summer break. As a coach, you're left hoping you've made a difference, that they've grown and gotten healthier under your watch. But you no longer see them everyday like you used to. You hope the values and lessons you've shared persist past the end of the season and carry your athletes through until the start of the next one.

Parents are also the ultimate role models, kind of like coaches but with a wider impact. Coaches show kids the ropes in their sports, making sure they "walk the walk" and not just "talk the talk." They set the example in a specific area. However, parents are role models in a bigger, nearly all-encompassing way. They don't just influence one or two behaviors; they shape their kids' entire view of the world. From little actions to demonstrating life values, the way parents behave and live their lives will mold how their kids grow and experience the world themselves. It's more than just teaching right from wrong; it's about setting the stage for their whole approach to life.

Parents and coaches also have an obligation to be fair. In coaching, being fair usually means making sure everyone gets a chance to play and is treated the same. It's all about giving each athlete a fair shot. But when you're a parent, fairness gets trickier. Sure, you want to be just, and treat your kids equally, but you also have to remember that each of your kids is different. They each have their own needs and situations. So, while you want to be fair, it doesn't mean treating them exactly the same. It's more about giving each kid what they need to thrive and feel supported.

Just like coaches, parents definitely need a break too. Everyone needs some time to relax and have fun. Coaches get their off-season to recharge, and parents should find ways to do the same. It's a good idea to mark downtime in the calendar. But also kids and families, just like teams, really benefit from doing fun stuff together. These leisure activities are all about having a great time and strengthening family bonds. No learning objectives needed – just pure enjoyment and making memories together.

Both parents and coaches want to see their kids and athletes grow to be successful and independent and to make smart choices on their own. Imagine the day when these young adults are facing the world without someone to guide them every step of the way. The goal is for all of the lessons to persist, even when no one's right there to give them a nudge in the right direction.

But Parenting Isn't Exactly Coaching

Although there are many similarities, there are also quite a few ways that coaching and parenting are different. Take giving feedback and criticism, for instance. It's a coach's job to zero in on how to improve a specific skill or behavior for the sport. It's all about performance. When parents give feedback, it's a whole different situation. Parents need to be careful of their child's feelings and be conscious of where they are in the process of growing up. It's more about gently guiding than pointing out what's wrong. Also, in families, it's important that feedback can go both ways. Parents should really listen to what their kids have to say and sometimes even think about changing how they do things based on that feedback. Coaches, on the other hand, don't typically need to have that kind of back-and-forth with their athletes.

Another big difference between coaching and parenting is how you handle your attitude and emotions when you're talking to your kids. In the sports world, coaches might get a bit fiery or show some anger to excite and rally their athletes. Sometimes that kind of energy can push athletes to do better. However, for parents, reaching that same level of fired-up isn't usually the most effective choice. As we'll explore more in this book, the way parents communicate is key. It's not just about the words you say, but also how you say them – your tone, the way you deliver your message, and even picking the right time and place to talk. All these things affect your child in big ways. As a parent, it's important to remember that your reactions can leave a lasting mark on how your kid sees themselves and on their emotional wellbeing.

When coaches tell athletes to learn from their mistakes they mostly mean mistakes made during the game or practice – things that affect how well the athlete plays the sport. In parenting, we're talking about a mix of life skills and growing a kid's character. So, when parents point out mistakes, it's more impactful if it's done in a caring way. What we really want is for our kids to become tough and resilient, and to be smart about their feelings – that's emotional intelligence. Teaching how to handle mistakes in parenting is more about guiding and supporting than just improving performance.

Some folks might think that motivating and encouraging kids is the same, whether you're a coach or a parent, but I see it differently. When coaches motivate, it's usually about hitting performance goals and winning games. It's like having a clear target to shoot at – score this many points, win this match. But in parenting, motivation takes on a different flavor. It's not just about winning or meeting goals. It's about helping your kids grow into great people. We're talking about cheering on their character development, getting excited about their hobbies and interests, and giving their confidence a boost. It's less about ticking off achievements and more about helping them grow in all areas of life in ways that best fit their personal goals, as well as your parenting goals.

Also, the approach toward discipline and structure needs to look pretty different for coaches as compared to parents. A coach has a specific area they're in charge of – on the field or the track. Parents have a much bigger area to manage. Parenting is about teaching the big stuff – values, life skills, and all the things kids need when they step into the world. When we talk about structure, we're not just talking about rules and bedtimes. It's about making a home that's safe, where kids feel cared for and supported. That's the kind of environment where they can really thrive.

Coaches give some emotional support, mostly about staying strong and focused in the game. They're there to help athletes handle the nerves and pressure when they're competing. But parents are like emotional support superheroes. They provide a kind of support that runs way deeper. Parents are there to help their kids through all sorts of stuff – the ups and downs, the happy times, and the tough ones. It's about really getting what's going on with their kids, not in one area, but in their whole lives. So, giving emotional support as a parent is a lot more involved and complex than what a coach must do. It's about being there, understanding, and guiding them through the whole emotional rollercoaster of growing up. Understand that providing emotional support as a parent is not just about being present for the emotional highs and lows; it's about navigating the intricate and often demanding journey of raising a child.

A Riley Story: My "Coaching" Parent

"Growing up, I found myself in a rather unique family dynamic, one that seamlessly merged the realms of parenting and coaching. My mother was a seasoned crisis intervention therapist. She now devotes her time as a school social worker. She and I are incredibly close and she is genuinely my best friend. I think she gives great advice, maybe because of her expertise in therapy and social working. On the other hand, for all of my life my father has been a head football coach for various high schools. Maybe I struck gold in the parent lottery because I get the benefit of being raised by both.

At first glance, you might expect a head football coach to be a stern and demanding parent, instilling discipline with an iron fist. Like it is mentioned in the chapter, parenting and coaching tend to differ in that way. When it comes to giving criticism and feedback, coaches are almost always going to be focused on the behavior and the specific skill needed for that sport. I am very happy to completely reverse that stereotype. Contrary to popular belief, my father's role on the field didn't translate into a tough or overbearing demeanor at home. He managed to strike a perfect balance between his coaching responsibilities and his role as a father. His advice was always delivered as guidance and not as demanding or correcting. His love for us is limitless, and he supports our endeavors with unwavering devotion.

One of the most valuable lessons my parents imparted upon us was the importance of exploration and self-discovery. Despite his profession, my father never imposed his athletic aspirations onto us. Instead, he encouraged us to pursue our passions, whatever they may be. This speaks for another contrast between parenting and coaching. Some people will say that motivation and encouragement is the same between coaching and parenting. When coaches motivate, it is more goal oriented, and the ultimate aim is to win a competition. Whereas motivating in parenting is more about encouraging character development, supporting various interests, and fostering their self esteem. As a result, my brothers found themselves drawn to the realms of music and art, nurturing their creative talents. As for me, I am a bit of a jack-of-all-trades, dabbling in everything from athletics to the arts and beyond.

In our household, there was never a shortage of encouragement or support from either of my parents. Whether we were chasing touchdowns or chasing melodies, our parents stood firmly behind us, cheering us on every step of the way. And while our paths may have diverged in terms of interests and pursuits, the bond we shared as a family remained unbreakable, grounded in love, respect, and an unwavering belief in each other's potential."

The Fundamental Dilemmas of Parenting

Parenting, with its unique demands and challenges, stands

apart from other roles like coaching or teaching. As we dive into the specific aspects that make parenting an especially tough job, let's explore what I refer to as the five dilemmas of parenting. These dilemmas highlight the distinct and sometimes daunting aspects of the parent-child relationship, setting it apart from other caregiving roles.

Let's be real, parenting is one tough gig. As someone who's been both a professor and a coach, I can tell you that parenting throws you some curveballs that those jobs never do. There are certain things in the whole parent-child dynamic that make the job ever more challenging. I like to think of these as the "Five Dilemmas of Parenting". These dilemmas are what make this a particularly difficult job, though, as I'll repeat often, still the toughest job you'll ever love.

The First Parenting Dilemma: Understanding the Constant Change

Here's the deal: the first big challenge in parenting is that your child is always changing. Whether they're in elementary school, high school, or college, they're going through developmental changes all the time. We don't need to get into heavy neuroscience, but it's interesting to note that science supports this. Neuroscientists have discovered that the decision-making part of the brain, known as the prefrontal cortex, is one of the last areas to fully develop. This part of the brain doesn't really settle down until the mid-20s, which is around the time we start to see a person's personality solidify. It is believed one's decision-making skills come into maturity around this age. If you've spent time with kids, tweens, teens, and young adults, you've likely noticed these constant changes yourself. It's a fascinating, ongoing process of growth and development.

A concern you may run into, or have already faced, is that what works for your child at one stage might not work at all down the road. It could even inflame a situation. That's why being a parent means you need to be flexible and switch up your strategies as your kids grow up. You might find yourself trying to stay one step ahead, anticipating and adapting to the changes as they come. It's a different arena for coaches and teachers, who don't necessarily have to make these constant adjustments. For parents, it's all about evolving alongside their children.

One thing that often flies under the radar is just how much the emotional world of your child or teenager expands. Your kid is going to start feeling a whole range of complex emotions. They'll ride the rollercoaster of mood swings, wrestle with questions of identity, and start recognizing and declaring their need for independence. This means your job as a parent gets more intricate. You're not just taking care of their physical needs; you also become an emotional resource and a confidant. You have to help them navigate these choppy emotional waters, which is a pretty significant part of parenting young adults.

Your young adult is going to go through a lot of changes – from their interests, to what they think is important, and maybe even who they hang out with. Their view of the world is going to keep updating, and sometimes it might take a different path from yours. As a parent, you've got to walk this fine line: staying connected with your kid and respecting their need to spread their wings. You'll have to find the delicate balance between being involved and giving them space.

While I've talked a lot about how kids and the world around them are constantly changing, there's another important piece to this puzzle: we, as parents, change too! It's crucial for parents to keep growing personally. This means doing some deep thinking about ourselves, chatting with others for different perspectives, and sometimes, even unlearning a parenting approach that's not working anymore. Change really is a massive part of life, and it's probably more of a challenge in parenting than in any other role. Adapting and evolving as a parent isn't just optional; it's part of the job description, as our kids and our world keep shifting.

The Second Dilemma: Less Time With You, More Independence

Here's something to chew on, which I call the second big parenting dilemma: As your kids grow older and more independent, they're going to spend less and less time hanging out with you. This shift brings its own set of challenges. For instance, as they spend more time outside the home, with friends or other activities, your chances for direct influence start to dwindle. Guiding them effectively can prove to be a bit of a tricky task when you're not seeing them as often.

As your kids start spending less time with you, they're spending more time soaking up the world on their own terms. This means they're often glued to screens, engaging with all sorts of media and technology. They're also getting most of their cues from friends, teachers, coaches, and other folks they meet. Here's the tricky part: sometimes the messages they're getting from these outside sources don't align with what you're trying to teach them at home. This clash of influences is what sits at the center of the second big dilemma of parenting. It's about navigating this imbalance, figuring out how to keep your values and lessons in play, even when you're not the only voice they're hearing.

When you're not spending as much time together, communication can get a bit bumpy. It's tougher to kick off those important heart-to-hearts when you're not seeing your child as often. You might find it harder to keep up with what's going on in their world – their thoughts, feelings, and what they're experiencing day-to-day. And let's face it, every engaged parent worries about their kid's safety when they're out and about. This is what makes the second dilemma a bit of a tightrope walk. It's a delicate dance, but getting it right is key to helping them (and you!) navigate this stage smoothly.

The Third Dilemma: Tackling Parenting as a Team

Here's the third big challenge in parenting: You're usually not doing it solo. Most of us are in this parenting gig with a partner, and guess what? They're also a parent to your child. There are situations where parents are going it alone and this dilemma may or not apply to them. However, parents who live in different households might find this applies to them. If you're co-parenting, almost invariably you will have some different ideas and philosophies about how to raise kids. Maybe they come from different backgrounds with totally different parenting styles. This mix can be a challenge – it takes a great deal of work to blend smoothly. If you don't make the effort to get on the same page, disagreements over parenting choices can spark conflict between you and your partner. But here's the kicker: it's not just about you. These disagreements can lead to mixed signals for your child. Kids need consistency. If the rules and discipline are all over the place, it can be confusing for them and might even lead to behavioral problems. That's why presenting a united front as parents is of the utmost importance. It's about finding common ground and sticking to it, for the sake of your child's wellbeing and your own peace of mind.

Another concern comes with dividing up the responsibilities. You have to figure out if you and your partner can split the parenting and household chores in a way that's fair. And what about finding time for each other? Parenting takes a lot of time and energy and can sometimes leave very little room for the couple's relationship. Not making time for each other can then lead to conflict or distance, which could lead to instability in the lives of your kids.

The solution to this dilemma is having those heart-to-heart

talks with your partner on something super close to both your hearts – your kids. Then, there's the part where you put all those decisions into action. But here's a key thing to keep in mind: your kids have their eyes on you. They're picking up on how you interact and work together. That's why it's so important for you as parents to show them what a healthy relationship looks like. It's not just about making good choices for your child; it's also about being a great example of teamwork and understanding in your partnership as well. Again, if you want this put more firmly, I recommend John Rosemond to you.

The Fourth Dilemma: Family History and Its Impact on Parenting

The fourth dilemma is about health and genetic factors from your family history. You'll want to stay one step ahead of health concerns and get clued in about any potential risks that might be lurking in the family tree. Sometimes, this might mean chatting with healthcare pros to get the full picture. Being the health detective for your family is yet another part of being a parent.

Sometimes families face difficult circumstances, like trauma from abuse, neglect, or serious hardships. This could even be something you, as a parent, have gone through, making your parenting journey even more unique and complex. And let's not forget about sibling dynamics – they're part of this mix too. This fourth dilemma is about not overlooking anything that may affect your child and your family. It's a big responsibility, and it may sound overwhelming, but it's all part of the parenting package.

Parenting, unfortunately, doesn't happen in a bubble. There's always a backdrop of family history and dynamics playing a role in your child's life. We're talking about patterns passed down through generations, and these can be good, or not-so-good. This could look like sticking to certain parenting styles just because "that's the way it's always been done" or "that's how my parents did it." Or this could look like dealing with and healing from generations of drug and alcohol problems or domestic abuse. Navigating this part of parenting means being aware that unhealthy family patterns, even from the past, can influence your parenting style and decisions. This means actively addressing what you want to carry forward and what you might want to change for your child's sake.

The Fifth Dilemma: Navigating the Heartbreaks of Parenting

Now, let's talk about the fifth and final dilemma. It's about dealing with heartbreak. As a parent, it's inevitable. You love this kid more than anything in the world, so when they hit rough patches, it hits you hard, too. Heartbreak isn't just about the big things; it's in those little moments of letting go. Like prying your preschooler's fingers off the car door on their first day of school, or waving goodbye as your teenager heads off to college. These moments are tough. Really tough.

Then there are the times when your child struggles – maybe with school, friends, or personal stuff. Watching them face these challenges can be incredibly hard. Your instinct might be to jump in and fix everything for them, but part of this dilemma is learning that they need to find their own way. Your role is to be their supporter, offering a helping hand and a listening ear, but not clearing every hurdle for them. Providing support while letting them grow and learn from their own experiences is a delicate balance.

Sometimes, your child's struggles will lead to disappointments and failures, and it's going to be heart-wrenching. No matter what area of life they struggle with, watching them face setbacks can really tug at your heartstrings. We'll explore this more later in the book, but one major goal for you as a parent is to help your child foster a growth mindset. It's about helping them see the value in effort and perseverance, even when things don't turn out perfectly right away. You might have heard some authors refer to this as building "grit", which is something that grows out of those very mistakes and failures. Helping your child develop this kind of resilience is one of the most challenging, yet rewarding, tasks as a parent. Stumbling isn't the end; it's just a part of becoming stronger and wiser.

It's kind of reassuring to know that you're not alone, right? Every parent throughout history has grappled with these same challenges. If you're sitting there, wondering, "How do I deal with all this?" Don't worry, that's exactly why we wrote this book. We're here to guide you through these dilemmas, offering tips, strategies, and a bit of wisdom to help you navigate the complex journey that is parenting.

An Erick Story: The Heartbreak I Can't Let Go, Even If He Can

"The night of the soccer banquet my son sat with his friends at the varsity table, eagerly waiting to hear his name called. He and his best friend had joined the team that season. They'd both played in lots of games in part because it was a small-roster team. However, I had noticed he had played less and less near the end of the season. It sometimes seemed like he'd play in one half but not the other. I was hoping getting a varsity letter would motivate him to work in the off-season. As the coach read off the names of the boys who had earned varsity letters they each stood up. When he led the audience in a round of applause I realized my son was the only one not standing. He sat perfectly still while the applause died down. My wife and I were shocked and then immediately heart broken. I tried to approach the coach after the banquet, but the only explanation I got was 'he didn't play enough.'

To my son's credit, he kept it together for the rest of the banquet. His disappointment and anger slowly came out on the ride home. My wife and I did our best to say the right things, but there were no right things. I myself almost cried in frustration and anger. Thank goodness my wife could stay calm.

We regrettably never talked about it again. I didn't have the courage to bring it up. My son and I didn't talk much in those days. Like all of my kids, there was a point in their teenage years when I became, according to them, 'the last person they wanted to talk to.'

I regret to this day that I never found the words to ask about it again. I didn't push through his resistance and figure out how he was doing.

He didn't play soccer again. To this day I'm convinced the coaches restricted his playing time specifically so he couldn't earn a letter. I learned later that earning a varsity letter came by playing in so many 'half's, not games.

The heartbreak you feel for your kid's sake can be intense, but we didn't go after the coach. We didn't let our anger allow us to make bad decisions. My wife counseled my son as best she could and we got through it. All of us learned how to grow. I've never brought it up again, and unless he reads this, he still doesn't know how I feel about that banquet. But I still don't talk to that coach."

CHAPTER 3 - HOW TO GUIDE YOUR YOUNG ADULT

Introducing the WISE ADULT Approach

I'd like to share what I think works. This method is the essence of everything I've experienced, researched in psychology, and gleaned from thousands of conversations with college students over my 35-year career. I've boiled it all down to something called the "WISE ADULT" approach. Don't get hung up on the acronym. It's just a handy way to keep track of your parenting goals and the strategies you might use to achieve them during your many talks with your child. So let's talk about communication.

Exploring Different Conversation Styles

Before we jump in, let's set the stage for younger parents who've not yet experienced the tweens, teens, or 20's. Be prepared. You're going to have a whole array of conversations with your child as they grow. I like to think these interactions can be sorted into different types, each having its own tone and objective. A lot of the time, these chats don't even feel like "parenting" in the traditional sense. The first point I want to make is that I'm not always steering the ship. Sometimes, I'm just cruising alongside my kids.

Understanding the five types of conversations reminds you that you can be many things to your child, depending on the situation. You're not stuck in the role of the strict disciplinarian or the law-setter, nor do you always have to be the joker or the fun-provider. As your child becomes more independent, you'll likely find yourself gravitating towards the first three conversational styles rather than the last two. It's all about adapting communication to fit the moment and your child's needs.

Mastering Parent-Child Conversations: From Heart-to-Hearts to Guiding Dialogues

Let's start with the first conversational style, which I like to call "just talking." Picture chatting with your kid as if they were a close friend. These talks are breezy and judgment free. You might be discussing simple things, like how their day was, the latest show they're into, or sharing a laugh over a funny incident. "Just talking" is all about sharing experiences and enjoying each other's company. It's less about having a goal and more about maintaining that heart-to-heart connection. My wife and I have found ourselves having more of these types of conversations with our kids as they've gotten older. And really, isn't this what every parent hopes for? Having those relaxed, easy chats where you're just enjoying being in each other's world.

The second type of conversation I call "sharing their successes." Think of it as letting them bring home their triumphs. Maybe it's a promotion at work, a successful project, acing a test, or excelling in a sport. Our job is pretty straightforward in these moments. We get to be their biggest fans. We can experience and share the joy of success and show them how proud and happy we are. Our goal is to help them feel truly appreciated and valued. However, I believe being an active listener is still important here. Ask questions, show your genuine interest, and encourage them to open up more about their experiences. These chats act as perfect opportunities to celebrate what they've achieved. Try to have as many of these as you can. Once they move out and start their own lives, you'll really start to miss these moments of shared joy and pride.

The third conversational style is "just listening." This is when your young adult is venting about something. Maybe frustrations in a relationship or challenges at work. There are times in their lives when they don't need advice or solutions; they just need someone to listen and understand, particularly during stressful or emotional periods. As parents, your role at these times is to offer empathy and understanding. Resist the urge to jump in with solutions, particularly as they get older. I know that will be tough, especially since you've been in charge of their lives for all of their life.

But in these talks your job is to validate their feelings. To let them know it's completely okay to feel upset, confused, or whatever they're feeling. And to reassure them that you're here for them. This can feel especially difficult in the tween and teenager years. Our instinct leads us to want to fix everything for them. I learned, particularly from my wife, that sometimes we just need to listen and not solve. As your child grows older, the need for these "just listening" conversations tends to increase, proving the value of practicing "just listening". As they get older, the problems sometimes get bigger. Learning to just listen doesn't always get easier.

The fourth type of conversation is more proactive than just listening. I call these the "gently guiding" talks. A big part of this book is dedicated to these kinds of conversations. Imagine your young adult is constantly upset about their job or overly critical of themselves. Here, your role might be to help them see things from a different angle. Reformulating a problem or just learning to put it out of one's mind is an incredibly powerful way to steer your child toward independence and success. This is where the concept of "reframing" comes into play.

"Gently guiding" talks need a delicate touch. You have to think carefully about what you want to achieve, while being sensitive to their feelings. You'll want to acknowledge what they're going through, but nudge them to consider other viewpoints. Even if they can't solve their problem right away, you can help them see that challenges often bring opportunities to learn and grow. This style of conversation is where your impact as a parent really starts to shine, especially as your kids mature.

We now come to the fifth type of conversation, which I call "heavy persuasion mode," or the classic "because I said so." This is when you need to have a serious talk about their actions or decisions. This talk is more than just shifting their attitude; it's about addressing something that could have real, lasting consequences. Maybe they're making choices that could harm them down the line, like overspending or ignoring important responsibilities. Or perhaps they're straying from family values. One key thing to master is how to have open, direct conversations without being critical. By non-critical, I mean focusing on the behavior instead of attacking their character. As you aim for raising an independent adult, remember: they're going to make choices you might not agree with. As they get older, managing difficult situations must become more about engaging in a dialogue rather than dictating a lecture. I certainly found the "because I said so" approach became less effective as they grew older. The challenging part is being receptive to their perspective, even if it differs wildly from yours. "Why can't you just think like me?" has no easy answer. They just don't. However, as a parent, there will be times when you need to assert your expectations firmly. You can balance a healthy respect for their autonomy with the necessity of clear guidance. I'll talk more about this later.

The bottom line in the art of parenting conversations is this: you're going to find yourself in all sorts of discussions, sometimes even shifting gears between different types within the same half-hour. However, it's crucial to understand that not every chat is a chance for you to drop wisdom or share your worldview. That's why I emphasize leaning more towards conversational styles one, two, and three, especially as your kids grow older. Less of the heavy-handedness of styles four and five. It is vital while we are growing young adults that we maintain mutual respect and trust. Your ability to communicate effectively will be put to the test when you're in the thick of a tough conversation with your child. Finding that balance between listening, guiding, and sometimes, just being there with them, is paramount. And remember, as they mature, the dynamic changes, as should your approach to these conversations.

A Haley Story: You Don't Need To Solve All Of Their Problems

"I've been extremely close with my mom for about 10 years. Once we got past my difficult teenage years, she and I fell into a rhythm of communication that, for the most part, works well and feels very natural to us. We are always honest with each other, always try to keep an open mind to one another's perspectives, and try to walk away from a conversation if it turns into a heated disagreement, since we are both very passionate and energetic individuals. My relationship with my father, however, is a bit of a different story. When I was in elementary school and high school, I rarely saw him, since he was always working late. My parents aren't separated or divorced, I just never had much down time to hangout with, chat with, or even really get to know my dad.

Oftentimes, as a kid, whenever I did get time with my dad, I'd try to vent about a situation or try to express how I felt about something that happened in school or with one of my friends. Without fail he would launch into a story about his own childhood, a work situation, or a similar narrative to try to connect. He'd trail off into long monologues that I did my best to try to absorb. I didn't always know how to apply his adult stories to my childhood problems, but

I still felt like he was trying. His default approach was always to lean in and try to fix the problem, immediately try to offer multiple solutions, or convince me it wasn't as bad as I might have been making it out to be. Often, our talks turned out to be a little too overwhelming to be productive. Needless to say, my connection with him suffered since I wasn't sure how to tell him what I needed from our talks as a younger kid.

Now, as an adult starting to figure out my way in relationships, I'm finding ways to connect with my dad and finding better techniques to communicate my needs. Communication styles should be flexible and serve different purposes throughout your child's development, as we've discussed, but they aren't always make or break when it comes to your emotional bond with your child. Don't worry so much about fixing your kid's situations. Sometimes they really just need a supportive shoulder or a sympathetic ear. Sometimes that sympathetic ear does so much more good than you could ever begin to imagine. There were so many times my mum sat near me while I ranted about something, only for me to realize halfway through exactly what it was that I needed to do to improve my situation. You are their first teacher, and the first person trusted with their life, wellbeing, and happiness. No matter how independent your child gets, that fact will never change. Don't be afraid to ask your kid what they think they might need from you and from different conversations as they grow up. Oftentimes, you'll both end up learning something about yourselves and each other, strengthening that parent-child bond even more."

Being Clear on What We Want to Achieve: The "WISE" Goals

How exactly do we navigate these diverse conversations with our kids? We can start by pinpointing the purpose of each conversation. As we've established, our goal is to guide our children into becoming independent, thriving adults. This means helping them develop good judgment and wisdom. This also means equipping them with the knowledge and tools they need to make their own sound decisions about their lives.

However, judgment and wisdom are not the same as being book-smart. Yes, judgment and wisdom require a combination of knowledge and skill. But it's also true that being "knowledgeable" doesn't automatically translate to making great choices. I agree. But my retort is that not knowing about a topic almost always leads to poor decisions. Our primary aim is to ensure our kids have the necessary knowledge and skills they need to navigate life. That's what this book focuses on. What do they need to know and be able to do?

So let's first ask "What does it mean to truly 'know' something?" More importantly, how do we lead someone toward "knowing" something? That's where the art of teaching comes into play. Understanding when someone genuinely "knows" something – to the point they can apply it to their life – is a crucial part of parenting. This book will offer insights on how to impart knowledge effectively, ensuring it sticks and eventually translates into wise decision-making.

To do that I've developed what I call the "WISE" goals. These represent the four critical stages of knowledge development and implementation. They act as milestones that show you whether your kid is truly ready to handle a specific topic. When they reach the final stage, that's your cue that they've got it covered. You can breathe a sigh of relief knowing they're prepared. Each stage is a stepping stone towards their understanding and ability to apply what they've learned in real-life scenarios. This progression is key to fostering their independence and readiness for the challenges ahead. But every learning moment begins with curiosity.

"W" - Willingness to Learn and Set Goals

The journey starts with "W" – the **Willingness to Learn and Set a Goal**. This is the launching pad for any subject or skill.

It all begins with a spark of curiosity and the desire to achieve something specific. Let's say you want your child to learn how to manage their finances. Your role is to kindle their interest and applaud their eagerness to learn. If you dream of them cooking their own healthy meals one day, start by nurturing their desire to cook and experiment with nutritious foods. Sometimes, your child's curiosity might veer towards something you're not too familiar with. That's perfectly fine. You can support them by providing books, enrolling them in courses, or finding a local mentor. In every aspect of thriving that we'll explore in this book, the first step in guiding your future adult is to encourage their curiosity and their willingness to learn. We can help light that initial spark that leads them down a path of discovery and eventual mastery.

"I" - Initiate and Implement

The **Initiate and Implement** stage is all about getting your child to set a practical goal and make their first moves towards it, even if it's just baby steps. You can encourage them to translate their willingness to learn into concrete action. If they're interested in managing finances, they could craft a budget, or maybe open a savings account. If they're excited about cooking, they could help plan meals, or contribute to the family grocery list.

What's key here is that they're applying what they've learned in a real-world context. Their first attempts probably won't be flawless – and that's perfectly okay. Your role is to cheer them on for taking these initial steps. It's these early efforts in "Initiating and Implementing" that pave the way to the next stages. Without these first steps, they can't progress further. So, celebrate their initiative and encourage their endeavors, because every big journey starts with these small but significant beginnings.

"S" - Sustained Practice

Our next step focuses on **Sustained Practice**. Once your child has started on their journey, the focus shifts to keeping the momentum going. This step is about reinforcing the idea that mastery and expertise come with consistent practice. If they've begun managing a budget, encourage them to stick with it. Teach them the value of watching their savings account grow without tapping into it prematurely. If cooking is their newfound interest, suggest they take charge of preparing several meals a week to solidify the habit.

Success in the "S" stage includes establishing routines or systems that make these positive behaviors more effortless, routine, and easier to maintain. The world is always changing, but the goal here is to help them continue practices that benefit them. We, as parents, can help them create a rhythm that supports their growth and helps solidify newly learned skills into enduring parts of their life.

"E" - Evaluate and Evolve

The **Evaluate and Evolve** stage is all about your child taking the reins of their own development. You know you've done your job when they're not just practicing what they've learned, but also actively looking for ways to adapt and grow. It's like they've become their own teacher, constantly seeking improvement and making adjustments as needed. Returning to our examples, in the realm of financial management they might regularly review their budget and explore new saving strategies. In terms of cooking and nutrition, they could choose to stay updated with the latest healthy cooking techniques and adapt to new dietary guidelines. This stage is about them being proactive. We want them to maintain what they've learned, but also expand their knowledge and adapt to new information. It's the point where they start to seek out learning opportunities on their own, signifying a true evolution into a self-sufficient, continuously improving individual.

When your child truly embodies the qualities of a "WISE" adult, it becomes evident in their ability to self-reflect and assess their own progress. This isn't just about achieving goals or mastering skills; it's about their capacity for adaptability, growth, and embracing change. They will start to ask themselves introspective questions and evaluate their journey. We want them to learn how to grow and adapt to the ever-changing world around them, and in response to their own shifting wants and needs.

I offer these four goals or stages because it's important to define our objectives before we embark on achieving them. These are the essential stages of learning that every student should progress through in any subject they study. We want our children to move all the way through "WISE".

Introducing the "ADULT" Method

How do we steer our kids to become "WISE" in the key areas of wellbeing we've talked about? The strategy I recommend is what I call the "ADULT" method. Think of it as a style of guiding or coaching that strikes the perfect balance between fostering independence and personal accountability, and being there when they need us. The "ADULT" method is essentially a pattern of conversation that you can apply to any of the wellbeing topics we'll explore. It's a sequential approach, designed to engage your child in meaningful dialogue and decision-making.

"A" is for "Ask"

When aiming to guide your teenager or young adult towards success in any area, the best starting point is to begin with an **Ask**. This step is important to help you gauge where they currently stand. What do they know, and what actions are they already taking? This step typically involves an open-ended question that invites them to share their perspectives, while you engage in active listening, demonstrating that you value their thoughts and opinions. This approach sets the stage for a judgment-free dialogue without jumping the gun with advice or conclusions. For instance, you might ask, "How do you feel about managing your own finances now that you're in college?" or "What's your take on cooking your meals? What kind of dishes do you like preparing?" The key here is that your question doesn't suggest any preconceived notions or that they've made a misstep. The aim is simply to have a relaxed, friendly conversation, similar to the ones mentioned earlier in the chapter. This is your way of subtly assessing whether they're "WISE" on the topic at hand. Depending on their response, the conversation might naturally progress to the second step.

"D" is for "Discuss and Dialogue"

The "D" in the "ADULT" method stands for **Discuss and Dialogue**. In this phase, your goal is to help your child explain their thoughts and ideas. You can use this step to help them better understand their reasoning and help them articulate their plans more clearly. Questions like "Have you thought about how to manage your monthly expenses?" or "What kind of meals do you think you can prepare in your dorm kitchen?" help in guiding this exploration. Sometimes, their responses might be spot-on, so there's no need for further probing. Our conversation can just continue on a friendly note. However, there might be instances where the dialogue extends, with them seeking information or clarification. In such scenarios, my approach is to hold back on offering solutions unless absolutely necessary. The aim is for them to figure things out independently as much as possible. If they don't need my input, we stick to this step.

It's crucial to understand that the goal is not to impose solutions. Let them steer the conversation. Ideally, they are the ones doing most of the diagnosing, with you acting merely as a sounding board. This way, they're not just receiving information; they're actively engaged in processing and applying it.

"U" is for "Up to You Suggestion"

If you notice that your child might not have fully analyzed the consequences of their choices, it might be time to transition to the third step, the **Up to You Suggestion**, which can also be thought of as the **Unforced Suggestion** since you're not going to use your authority to impose this solution upon them. This part of the conversation might look like this: "This is completely up to you, and I'll support whatever you decide, but have you thought of…"

There are tactful ways to offer a suggestion without making it feel forced. Later in the book, we'll explore more examples, but here are a few to consider:

> "I have a thought that might be helpful. Would you like to hear it?"
> "May I suggest an idea that we could explore together?"
> "Based on what you've shared, I have an idea. Would you be interested in hearing it?"

I confess I've gotten these kinds of opening lines from "motivational interviewing," a dialogue technique designed to help people change behavior. I recommend learning more about this process if you wish to really dig into how to persuade or nudge people into change.

The critical part of this third step is to present suggestions gently, leaving the ultimate decision in the hands of your young adult. Your aim isn't to sway their choice, but offering a new choice or strategy. An alternative perspective can prove invaluable in preparing them for independent problem solving. It's crucial to frame these as options, not commands. The phrase

"This is completely up to you" is key – it signals that, while you have an input to share, the decision is completely theirs to make. This way, you're contributing to the conversation without overriding their autonomy.

Let's consider additional practical examples of how to use "Up to You Suggestions." You might say, "I've come across some budgeting strategies for students. Would you be interested in hearing about them?" or "I found some easy and healthy recipes online. Do you want to take a look together?" These are gentle nudges that invite your young adult to explore new ideas without feeling pressured.

Another approach is to share a relevant personal experience. Your story should still be framed as a suggestion instead of a command, but a personal story can often offer an alternative. For example, "I once faced a similar challenge and tried this approach. It might be something that could work for you too. What do you think?"

Reflecting on this style of conversation, you'll likely realize that it's quite similar to how you interact with friends. Offering suggestions, in a polite, non-intrusive manner, is a common way adults communicate with each other. Applying this same approach with your young adult can be effective. It respects their growing independence and treats them like the adults they are becoming. By engaging this way, you're not just instructing; you're empowering them to make informed decisions and build their own sense of responsibility.

"L" is for "Lean In"

When the first three steps don't quite hit the mark, it's time for the fourth stage, where you might need to **Lean In** a bit more assertively. This is where you adopt a more persuasive tone, something akin to your role as a parent in their earlier years, yet with a few differences. For instance, you might say, "I really think tracking your expenses could be a big help. There are some great apps out there for budgeting. Here's a few I found." Or "Cooking your own meals can be both fun and healthy. I think we should try to make something together this weekend."

In this step, you do sound more like the traditional parent – the one who used to make most of the decisions. However, the difference with your young adult is that this needs to be more of a dialogue. Be prepared to hear their side of the story. They might have valid reasons for their actions or inactions. While you can present your viewpoint, remember, unless it's a matter of safety, you might need to give them space to try things their way.

This conversation style can be challenging, especially when you're inclined to have your way. However, keeping the ultimate goal in mind is crucial. If your child is to become a "WISE", thriving, independent individual, they need to learn to make these decisions themselves. As they grow older and move out, your role will have to shift to more persuasion than direction. In my experience with my own children, who are now in their late 20s and early 30s, I find myself rarely reaching this "L" stage anymore. It's a sign of their growing autonomy and my evolving role as a parent.

"T" is for "Third Party"

Finally, we arrive at step five: "T" for **Third Party** or **Trained Expert**. Let's face it, none of us knows everything. With the constant emergence of new technologies and novel challenges, it's unrealistic to think we can be the sole source of wisdom for our children in every aspect of life. Sometimes, the most effective approach is to guide them towards a third party or an expert in the field, especially if they haven't fully embraced being "WISE" in a particular area yet and are not inclined to reach out to someone on their own.

Referencing someone new might also make sense during those times your child is not receptive to your advice. In such cases, suggesting a third party could be a strategic move. As an example, you might say, "Perhaps chatting with Uncle Joel about financial planning would be helpful for you?" or "How about joining a cooking class to pick up some new skills? Let's see what's available nearby." When specialized knowledge or skills are required, guiding them to seek expert advice can be your best bet. And it's OK that we don't know something. We should want our kids to outsmart us. In fact, we should wholeheartedly hope they do. Encouraging them to learn from others and expand their horizons is a part of helping them grow into well-rounded, informed adults.

Navigating the Future with the "WISE" Goals and "ADULT" Methods

Parenting is hard work. It requires adaptation, empathy, knowledge, communication skills, etc... I'm not pretending I'm going to cover everything in this book. The "ADULT" method offers a way to continue guiding and coaching your young adult, while simultaneously respecting and fostering their independence. The "WISE" goals act as a compass in these conversations. They help you identify your objectives and provide a framework to gauge your kids' understanding and actions regarding various topics. I find that distilling concepts into acronyms like "WISE ADULT" makes them more accessible and easier to recall when we need them. These acronyms aren't just catchy; they're tools to help us navigate the parenting journey more effectively. As we move into the next chapters, we'll apply the "WISE ADULT" method across each of the five wellbeing categories. This approach isn't about having all the answers, but about having the right mindset and tools to support our children's growth in an ever-changing world. I've said it often - parenting is the toughest job you'll ever love! Let's get started.

An Erick Story: Mom And Dad Can't Always Be There

*"Recently my youngest son moved from South Carolina to Colorado. We live near Pittsburgh, so this was a significant jump in distance. He went to take a new job and didn't know anyone except a cousin he'd seen maybe 10 times in his life. This cousin was busy raising three kids, so it wasn't like she was going to entertain him or show him around. As the first month dragged into the second, he started getting sick. Bouts of nausea and stomach upset happened on and off for two weeks. He even missed several days of work. He described it as someone kicking him in the stomach. With each phone call we would start with an **Ask**, 'How are you feeling today?' This would always lead to a **Dialogue** about what happened recently. We didn't have any clue why this kept coming back, but he speculated it was because of his bad diet, so he made some changes. But things were very busy at work. When the pains came back again very quickly he'd tell us it was probably because he couldn't stick to his diet. We made some **Up to You Suggestions** about what we thought were the healthiest changes to his diet. But, in one call, I also **Leaned In**. I suggested another visit to a doctor if it kept coming back. He didn't formally agree with my suggestion but he'd heard me plenty of times say 'go see a doctor.' He knew where I stood.*

*A couple days later he explained he'd been to urgent care and they thought he was constipated. All of the changes he'd made to his diet were actually the wrong ones. Turns out increasing your fiber in some cases only backs up the system more. We said we couldn't really help much and that we were glad he'd gone to a **Trained Expert**. We were very happy he was being proactive. He changed his diet again and we waited to see if things would clear up.*

A few days later he called to say he was in the Emergency Room. His severe pains had come back. He'd been throwing up for nearly 24 hours and nothing was in his system. The doctor said he was having reduced kidney function. He got a CT scan and I distracted him on the phone for 30 minutes while he waited for the results.

We were concerned it might be something long term. We had a laundry list of things that our friends or neighbors had suggested it could be. We were particularly bummed that we couldn't be there and that he had to drive himself to the hospital. We wondered how he might get his truck home if he couldn't drive when they released him. Importantly, we made sure to share with him that we thought he'd done the right thing to go to the ER. It sounded like his symptoms were serious and he wasn't getting better.

When he called back he explained he had been diagnosed with a kidney stone. Funny, that option had never occurred to either of us. The hospital gave him medication and plenty of IV fluids. After a couple of weeks of observing the kidney stone and it didn't pass they finally did an outpatient procedure and went and got it. My son is feeling fine now.

I'm glad we were on the phone with him several times, but ultimately, my son took care of himself. It was his call to go to urgent care, and when things got worse, he drove himself to the ER. He had his insurance card, knew his medical history, and could describe his symptoms well enough to get the right tests done. He's healthy and back to enjoying his new city. I guess this was the best possible outcome. He got sick and he took care of himself. That's the best we can do."

CHAPTER 4 - RAISING A HEALTHY ADULT

As a parent of a teenager, you know how quickly things change. Their bodies, their minds, and their emotions are all in fast-forward, and keeping up can be tough. But one thing that remains constant is the importance of their health. In this chapter, we're diving into some essential health topics tailored just for your young adult. We'll explore five key fitness measures that are pillars for anyone's wellbeing. These aren't about heavy gym sessions or running marathons; instead, they're simple, everyday checks to ensure your body is staying balanced, from your heart rate to how much you can stretch.

Then, we'll shift gears and talk about modern medicine. It's not just about popping pills when sick; it's about understanding what's helpful and what's not, and when to seek advice from professionals. It's crucial for your young adult to know the value of medicine and the importance of using it wisely, respecting both its power and its limitations.

I also point out that physical health and mental health are two sides of the same coin. You can't have one in tip-top shape without the other. We'll guide you through straightforward strategies to ensure your young adult's body is healthy so their mind can be too. It's about creating harmony between the physical and the mental, ensuring they complement each other rather than compete.

Lastly, stress is another biggie. It's like the shadow that follows everyone around, especially during the young adult years. We'll break down what stress really is, how it affects the body and mind, and most importantly, how to manage it. It's not about avoiding stress—that's impossible—but about equipping your young adult with the tools to handle it, to keep it from overwhelming them, and to use it in ways that can actually be beneficial.

This chapter is packed with practical advice, grounded in the latest research, yet presented in a way that's easy to digest and apply. At the end of the day, we all want the same thing: to see our young adults grow up to be healthy, happy, and thriving, ready to tackle whatever comes their way with confidence and resilience. I want to equip you with the knowledge and tools to support your teen in mastering the art of maintaining their health, both inside and out.

Discovering Fitness: The Five Key Measures

There are five main things that contribute to measuring how fit you are. Everyone from physical therapists to gym instructors use these measures. I wish I'd known about them earlier than my 50's and I really wish I'd taught my kids about them too. However, thank goodness, it's never too late to learn.

Cardiovascular Endurance

The first measure of physical fitness is something you've probably heard of – "cardiovascular endurance." This is all about how well your heart, lungs, and blood vessels team up to keep you moving and healthy. I like to think of it as how efficiently your body gets oxygen to your cells, though, that's a pretty simplified way of phrasing it. Now, I'm not going to dive into all the science-y details here – you can easily find that info online. The main thing to remember is this: if you're not getting your heart and lungs working with some cardio exercises now and then, they gradually lose their oomph. Just like any muscle, your heart needs a regular workout to stay strong, and your lungs need it to stay clear and healthy. Whether it's cycling, jogging, or playing a sport like volleyball, doing some form of regular cardio is key. For our kids, it's crucial they keep this up through their lives, ideally more than just once a week.

Muscular Strength

Next up is "muscular strength." Now, hold on, I'm not saying we all need to aim for Mr. Universe here, but keeping your muscles in good shape is important. It's not just about lifting heavy weights at the gym – although, a little weight lifting is great for your bones, too. You don't need to worry about setting records. It's more about making sure you're challenging your major muscle groups regularly. If not, you might find yourself on a slow slide into muscle weakness. And here's a cool idea – you can actually hit two goals with one activity. For example, why not suggest your young adult join a gym or a sports league? It's a great way to stay fit, and they might even make some new friends along the way. A big step toward maintaining muscular fitness can be to find fun, engaging ways to build strength while maybe even adding a social element.

Muscular Endurance

Let's talk about the third fitness measure: "muscular endurance." This one's a bit different from muscular strength. It isn't about how much weight your muscles can move, but how well they can perform repeated movements or hold a position for a long time. Think about exercises like push-ups, sit-ups, or squats, or how long you can hold a plank. These are all about endurance. How do you keep up this kind of fitness? Well, it's in the name – you've got to do these exercises over and over again. Muscular endurance can be built in more ways than just running or playing volleyball. Sometimes, you might need a bit more structure, like getting a workout instructor or joining a fitness class, especially if doing these exercises at home feels like an uphill battle. We need to find ways to challenge those muscles consistently.

Flexibility

Measure number four is all about "flexibility." This one checks how much your bones, tendons, and muscles can move around each joint. Speaking from personal experience, especially with my chronic back issues, I'm always working on keeping my back flexible. Many of us who are a bit older know just how crucial flexibility is in our daily lives. Here's the thing, though: our young, spry kids probably aren't thinking about this much. Like many things, flexibility decreases as we age, and it's important for them to know that. Down the line, they'll need to incorporate a regular stretching routine to stay limber. We're not saying everyone needs to aim for gymnast-level flexibility or become a yoga pro, but it's smart to realize that maintaining flexibility gets tougher over time. So, getting a jump start on good flexibility habits early on is a wise move.

Body Composition

The last, but definitely not the least, measure of physical fitness is "body composition." This one is all about the ratio of fat to lean muscle mass in your body. Sure, weight is part of the equation, but there's more to it. Talking about body composition with your kids can be tricky. There's a great deal of sensitivity around the topic, especially with concerns about "fat shaming" if they're on the heavier side, or worries about being too skinny. I would recommend leading the conversation with disclaimers that you don't want to talk about the numbers on the scale or how they look. Focus on how maintaining a healthy body composition is crucial for physical and mental health, energy levels, and long-term wellbeing. Reinforce that everyone's body is unique and that health is not about fitting into a specific size or shape. Encourage them to appreciate what their body can do and promote a mindset of gratitude for their body's capabilities. Importantly, create an environment where your young adult feels comfortable discussing body composition and health. Listen actively, respond without judgment, and provide reassurance that you support them. The key is to educate your kids about this measure without causing them stress or obsession. It's a fine line to walk.

If there are issues or concerns about body composition, it's a good idea to seek professional advice. The simple old Body Mass Index (BMI) is no longer considered the best gauge for body composition, so it's worth looking into more accurate and healthy ways to understand and manage body composition.

When it comes to these five fitness measures, recognize that they're never one-size-fits-all. Each of our kids is unique, and their fitness goals and abilities will vary. What's right for one might not be the same for another. If you want your kids to be physically healthy, they need to understand how fitness is actually measured. It's not just about hitting the gym; it's about knowing what counts in fitness and why.

So, how do you teach your kids about these five measures in a way that sticks? That's where our WISE ADULT method comes into play. Let's break it down and see how we can use this approach to guide our children towards understanding and valuing physical fitness, tailored to their own paths and capabilities.

Setting WISE Goals for Physical Fitness

To kick things off, let's use the WISE framework to set our goals around physical fitness for our young adults. Our main aim is to spark their interest in fitness and encourage them to set personal fitness goals. If you haven't really talked about fitness with your kid, or they haven't shown much interest yet, our first target is **Willingness to Learn and Set a Goal**. This might mean linking their future wellbeing and success to being physically fit. Using personal anecdotes or examples from close family members can be a good conversation starter.

Once we see that they're willing to learn and have a fitness goal in mind, we can help them move to **Initiate and Implement**. Are they regularly getting some exercise, stretching, or doing activities that challenge their cardiovascular endurance? Then, we'll check if they're meeting the **Sustained Practice** goals. This is about whether they have a regular fitness routine and are keeping track of their exercises, aiming to improve in all five fitness measures.

Lastly, when we see that fitness has become a part of their lifestyle, our focus shifts to **Evaluate and Evolve**. They can't just stick to one routine forever. They should stay open to new fitness ideas and updates, learning from both peers and experts. If we see them actively evolving their fitness habits, we can be confident that they're taking good care of their physical health, and our role as a guide in this aspect has been successful.

The ADULT Method for Physical Fitness

Achieving these fitness goals with our young adults is where the **ADULT** method comes into play. Think of it as a roadmap for the ongoing conversations about fitness you'll have with your young adult. This method is flexible – you can pause at any stage if it feels right, or you can extend the conversation over multiple interactions. It's not about rushing to tick all the boxes in one go.

Starting with **Ask** is all about gently probing your young adult's interest and awareness in fitness. You could open with remarks like, "I've noticed you're paying more attention to your health and fitness," or a question like, "How do you feel about your physical activity levels?" This is a soft way to kickstart a dialogue, possibly leading to deeper discussions as part of the **ADULT** method. Or, it might not. That's okay too. The goal here is simply to find out whether fitness is something they're even thinking about.

If fitness is on their radar, you can continue with more focused questions. Have they started a fitness routine? Are they familiar with the five key measures of physical fitness? Do they recognize the importance of stretching as they age? Are they aware that managing their physical fitness will be their responsibility? Positive responses to these questions can lead you to inquire about their **Sustained Practice**. Are they consistently engaging in fitness activities? And finally, you might discuss the need to **Evaluate and Evolve** their fitness habits over time, ensuring they understand the importance of adapting their routines as they grow and change.

When we find out that our young adults aren't quite on track with the **WISE** goals for physical fitness, it's time for **Dialogue and Discussion**. The focus here isn't about changing their minds or directing them; it's invaluable to have open conversations, just like you would with a friend. This is the stage where you don't make suggestions or dictate actions. In fact, you might discover that they know more about certain aspects of fitness than you do – and that's fantastic! Let them take the lead in the conversation; it's a great confidence booster and promotes learning.

The key objective as a parent is to gauge if they have enough understanding of fitness for their age and stage in life. This understanding varies significantly if they're just entering high school or preparing to move out. Over time, you'll hopefully reinforce these concepts, nurturing their ownership of their fitness journey.

The main question to explore in these discussions is whether they're actively using their knowledge of fitness. Are they initiating and implementing activities to improve their fitness? Are they sticking to a workout schedule or started planning healthy meals? Depending on your child's age, you might find that everything is already on track, and they're exactly where they should be in terms of their fitness understanding and practices. If that's the case, congratulations – your guidance has been successful, at least for now!

If you find out that your child might not be as up-to-speed with physical fitness as they should be for their age, or if they're lacking in certain fitness areas, it's time to move to the "**U**" step of our method – **Up to You Suggestion**. Here, we shift from just asking and discussing to gently offering help. The nature of "suggestions" changes depending on your child's age and the situation. While "because I said so" might work for younger kids sometimes, it's not going to work as well for teenagers or college-aged young adults. At this stage in their lives, it's vital that they start making healthy decisions for themselves. They shouldn't be reliant on you to decide everything for them.

With an **Up to You Suggestion** you're looking to provide guidance without imposing it. You might ask if they've considered trying out for a new sport or a fitness class. Have they considered establishing a regular workout schedule? This approach has to do with encouraging them to make their own choices and learn from those decisions. You should be focused on presenting options and reinforcing ideas that your young adult may have already expressed. Remember, the key is to make each suggestion feel unforced and respectful of their independence. This aligns with the techniques we explored in Chapter 3 about offering choices. For instance, you could say, "Based on what you shared, I have an idea. Would you be interested in hearing it?" or "If you're open to it, I'd like to suggest something about fitness that my friend Sally found useful. Would that be OK?" By using phrases like "up to you," you're clearly signaling that while you're providing advice, the final decision, and the responsibility that comes with it, is theirs.

When faced with what you perceive as unhealthy, or even dangerous behavior in your young adult, it's time to employ the "**L**" step of the **ADULT** method – **Lean In**. However, when dealing with young adults, persuasion is more effective than ultimatums. This book doesn't dive too deep into the art of persuasion, but as a parent who has been with them throughout their lives, you likely have a good understanding of which approaches resonate with them and which won't.

Initiating this kind of conversation can often be the most challenging part. For example, I've found that when I bring up the topic of fitness with one of my kids, they immediately resist and accuse me of fat shaming. Despite their resistance, these conversations are essential. It's not about wanting them to look a certain way or about achieving specific athletic feats; it's about ensuring they understand the importance of taking responsibility for their own fitness throughout life. It's crucial to find out how they perceive this challenge and whether they feel prepared to meet it. In these situations, the conversation is less about laying down the law and more about opening a dialogue. As parents we can offer insights and perhaps gently guide them to see the value in making healthier choices. The goal is to encourage them to think critically about their health and fitness and empower them to take control of their wellbeing.

When it comes to the **Lean In** step, we can also think of it as **Lead to Persuade**. The older our kids get, the less commanding we become, and the more they take the reins of their own lives. Deciding when to use **Lean In** or **Lead to Persuade** is a judgment call that varies with each situation and child. The great part is that this doesn't need to be a one-off talk. It's more effective to spread it out over time, letting the conversation about physical fitness build gradually.

We, as the more experienced generation, understand the profound impact of physical fitness on our quality of life. Being sick or unhealthy can drastically alter our day-to-day experiences. Hopefully, we're acting as role models for our children in terms of fitness. It's never too late to start setting a good example. However, even if we don't feel like we've been the best role models, we shouldn't shy away from discussing fitness with our children. We need to ensure they understand the importance of being responsible for their physical wellbeing, regardless of their parents' fitness journeys.

When we reach a point where our expertise falls short, or when our young adults are reluctant to discuss certain topics with us, it's time to embrace the"**T**" in the **ADULT** method – referring them to a **Third Party** or a **Trained Expert**. In the realm of fitness, this often means seeking advice from fitness professionals or, in more challenging cases, consulting medical experts.

In today's world, where information is abundant, but not always accurate, discerning the right source of guidance becomes crucial. Especially because your kids are likely seeing a huge amount of fitness influencer content across various social media platforms. Finding the right guidance for your child might involve doing some research to find credible and reliable fitness resources. With your help they can learn to navigate through the maze of fads, advertising motives, and misinformation that saturates our information landscape.

Remember, you don't have to be an expert in every aspect of fitness to have meaningful conversations about it. Your role isn't to have all the answers, but to guide your young adult towards taking responsibility for their own fitness. Helping them become **WISE** about fitness involves acknowledging when it's time to bring in external expertise. We are capable of helping to equip them with the tools and resources they need to someday maintain their health independently.

Embracing the **ADULT** method in your parenting approach can indeed feel a bit awkward initially. It's not to say that you can't have spontaneous, varied types of conversations with your child. However, this method offers a structured way to foster autonomy and encourage self-reliance in your young adult.

The beauty of the **ADULT** method lies in its ability to clearly define what we want our children to learn and how to practically apply this knowledge. It aims to empower them to make wise decisions based on their understanding and capabilities. The **WISE** goals set the foundation for what we want them to achieve, while the **ADULT** method provides a roadmap to reach these objectives. Repeatedly using these methods can significantly contribute to raising a successful, independent adult. But remember, these aren't rigid frameworks. They are designed to be flexible and adaptable to different situations and stages of your child's development. The key is to use it as a guiding tool, adjusting it as needed to fit your child's unique needs and responses. This adaptability makes the **ADULT** method a valuable and dynamic approach in the ever-evolving journey of parenting.

Embracing Modern Medicine: A Must for Young Adults

Today, a significant challenge for many young adults is understanding how to properly utilize the medical community. Some have a stubborn reluctance to visit a doctor. But, in my view, this attitude leads them to miss out on a crucial aspect of wellbeing. We're living in an era with the most advanced medicine ever known, in this country right at our fingertips. Ignoring the benefits of modern medical care, both for physical and mental health, is certainly a missed opportunity.

There are various reasons why young adults, and even parents, hesitate to seek medical advice. Concerns about stigma, past negative experiences, or familial beliefs can all play a role. However, we're addressing this topic directly because looking after physical and mental health is one of the simplest ways to enhance our quality of life.

Unless you're a trained and licensed healthcare professional, chances are you don't know as much as the professionals do about health. There might be gaps in your knowledge that you aren't even aware of. For instance, did you know that the range of conditions treatable by medical and behavioral health specialists has significantly expanded recently? The medical insights and practices from your childhood might not hold true anymore.

It's crucial not to let hesitations prevent your child from exploring the options available through the medical community. Behavioral health and medical care have evolved tremendously, and they offer invaluable resources for maintaining and improving health. So, don't shy away from giving them a chance to contribute positively to your kid's life.

If your future young adult is already showing reluctance towards seeking medical help, it's vital to understand why. Are they afraid, lacking trust, or carrying baggage from previous negative experiences? Identifying the root cause of their hesitation is your first step, and here's where the **ADULT** method can really make a difference. Start by reassuring them about the confidentiality of doctor-patient conversations and emphasize their autonomy in making healthcare decisions. They should understand that regular check-ups and preventive care are critical for catching health issues early, potentially preventing more severe problems down the line.

Your support will be crucial in this process. Sometimes, accompanying them to appointments can make a significant difference. Also, finding a doctor they feel comfortable with can change their entire perspective on healthcare. As your child grows older and transitions off your health insurance policy, it's a good idea to check in and ensure they don't neglect their health needs. This might mean exploring and discussing affordable healthcare options with them. Remember, the goal is to guide them to take proactive steps in managing their health, making informed decisions, and understanding the importance of regular medical care.

Starting the Conversation: Encouraging Young Adults to Visit the Doctor

Initiating a conversation about visiting the doctor with your young adult can begin with a simple, empathetic question. For example, gently ask, "I've noticed you seem a bit hesitant about going to the doctor. Would you like to talk about it?" This opens up a dialogue in a non-threatening way, showing that you're there to listen and that you want to understand their concerns.

Another approach is to share information to spark their interest. You might say, "I recently read about how regular health checkups become more important as we age. Would you be interested in talking about that together?" This can lead to a productive discussion about the importance of proactive health care. Sometimes, sharing your own experiences can make the topic more relatable. You could try saying, "I understand that going to the doctor can be uncomfortable. I feel that way too, sometimes. But I found that it has really helped me stay healthy. Can I share some of my experiences with you?" This approach shows empathy and provides a personal touch to the conversation.

When guiding young adults in understanding and managing their health, there are several key aspects they need to be aware of. This includes recognizing the value of preventive care and being proactive about their health needs.

Firstly, you'll want your kids to understand the importance of routine preventive care. This includes scheduling their annual physical exams and necessary health screenings. Preventive care plays a crucial role in early detection and effective management of various health conditions. It's not just about going to the doctor when they're sick; this concerns regular check-ups to maintain their overall health and catch potential issues early.

Secondly, a critical area they need to grasp is the significance of mental health and its parity with physical health. They should know when it's appropriate to seek professional help for emotional and mental challenges. Recognizing the signs that indicate a need for mental health support is vital. We will explore this topic more extensively in a later section.

Additionally, they should have a basic understanding of the mental health profession's structure. This includes knowing the differences and roles of therapists, counselors, and support groups, among others. Understanding these distinctions will help them navigate the mental health system more effectively when they need support.

Encouraging young adults to be proactive in their healthcare conversations is key. They should feel empowered to ask questions and understand their health conditions fully. It's also important for them to know that seeking second opinions is a normal and often necessary part of making informed healthcare decisions.

Ultimately, self-advocacy in healthcare is crucial. Young adults need to learn how to stand up for their own health needs and understand their rights within the healthcare system. This means being informed about their health conditions, treatment options, and being able to communicate their needs and preferences to their healthcare providers effectively.

By fostering these skills and understandings, we help young adults take control of their health, make informed decisions, and ensure they receive the care they deserve. This empowerment is a significant step towards their overall wellbeing and independence.

WISE Goals for Engaging with the Medical Community

For young adults, appropriately utilizing the medical community to maintain their physical, mental, and emotional health involves a series of steps defined by the **WISE** goals. **'W'** for **Willingness to Learn** is the foundational step. It's all about developing a mindset that values health and wellness. It involves being open and eager to learn about various aspects of health care. From understanding how the healthcare system works to recognizing their own personal health needs and the resources available to them. This step also entails staying updated on health-related topics and modern medical advancements. Our young adults need to know how to set a proactive goal to engage with and utilize behavioral health and medical services. Encouraging your young adult to be willing to learn involves discussing the importance of health, sharing resources, and even setting an example through your own attitudes towards health and wellness. By fostering a **Willingness to Learn** you're helping your young adult see the importance of being informed and proactive about their health, laying the groundwork for a lifetime of healthy habits and informed health care decisions.

In the **Initiate and Implement** of the **WISE** goals, young adults take a crucial step in actively managing their health by engaging with the healthcare system. This phase is all about action. They begin scheduling their own regular health checkups and screenings, taking charge of their physical health through preventive care. It's not just about responding when they feel unwell; it's a proactive approach to health maintenance. Additionally, they also start recognizing and utilizing mental health resources when necessary. Whether it's seeking counseling for emotional challenges or finding support for mental wellbeing, this step is about acknowledging the need for help and actively seeking it out. Essentially, **Initiate and Implement** is the transformative phase where knowledge and willingness turn into concrete health-promoting actions.

In the **Sustained Practice** phase of the **WISE** goals, the focus is on maintaining a consistent engagement with the healthcare system. This is where young adults establish and nurture a trusting relationship with a healthcare professional in their community, someone who is well-acquainted with their long-term health journey. This doesn't just refer to occasional visits; this step involves actively forming a partnership with a medical professional who plays an active role in their ongoing health.

Moving to the "E" phase, **Evaluate and Evolve**, the emphasis shifts to a continuous assessment of their health needs and adapting their healthcare strategies as necessary. This is particularly important as they age and undergo various lifestyle changes. It involves the ability to reevaluate and modify their health care approaches in response to evolving health requirements. Whether it's altering their fitness routine, adjusting their diet, or changing their mental health support strategies, this stage is all about flexibility and adaptation to ensure their health regimen remains effective throughout different stages of life.

Applying the ADULT Method to Utilizing the Medical System

Starting with **Ask**, the conversation might begin with inquiries about their current health and wellness management. You could ask, "How do you feel about your current health and wellness? Are you comfortable with how you're managing it, including regular checkups and mental health?" This opens the door for them to express their views and concerns, setting a tone for an open and non-judgmental discussion.

If they haven't yet reached the "E" goal of **Evaluating and Evolving** their health status, you can move to **Dialogue**. Here, you might ask questions like, "Have you thought about what steps you might take if you ever felt overwhelmed?" or "Have you ever considered the importance of preventive health care?" This step aims to encourage them to think more deeply about their health and wellness strategies.

In cases where you see an opportunity to make an **Up to You Suggestion**, you could offer insights or resources in a non-intrusive manner. For instance, "It's completely up to you, but I read an interesting article about the connection between physical exercise and mental health. Would you like me to share it with you? It could offer some useful perspectives."

There might be times when it's appropriate to **Lean In** a bit more. You could say, "I really think establishing a strong relationship with a doctor is important. Have you thought about finding a doctor or therapist you're comfortable with?"

Finally, there will be instances where the best approach is to recommend a **Third Party** or **Trained Expert**. In such cases, you might suggest, "Do you know when it's time to consult a healthcare professional? They can offer tailored advice. Would you like some help in finding a reliable one?"

Navigating the complex world of health-related issues with your young adult can be daunting, especially considering the wide array of potential concerns they may encounter. That's why fostering the right attitude and judgment about when to seek healthcare is crucial. We can't just address specific health problems as they arise; it's paramount to instill a proactive mindset towards health and wellness in your young adult. Starting these conversations can vary in approach, depending on your relationship and the individual circumstances. The key is to ensure that by the time they move out of your home, they are not hesitant or unwilling to consult a doctor or therapist when needed. It's important to communicate that seeking professional health care is a normal, responsible, and an essential aspect of taking care of oneself. The consequences of neglecting health can be serious, and in some cases, even disastrous. By having open, honest, and supportive discussions about health, you can help your young adult understand the value of regular health check-ups, mental health care, and timely medical intervention. The goal is to prepare them to independently manage their health, recognizing when professional help is needed and feeling comfortable in seeking it out.

A Riley Story: You're Never Too Young (Or Old) For Therapy

"When I was younger, I became involved in a toxic relationship. I was juggling my first job, friendships, a relationship, school, and extracurricular activities. A lot to keep up with for anyone, let alone at a young age. If there was a high moment in the relationship, it was quickly dragged down by the weight of mental abuse. This individual was very manipulative, and gaslit me into thinking that was the way love was supposed to be. I didn't know any better. I had great guidance from my family and friends, but when it came to red flags, I became colorblind. His behavior became normalized in my eyes.

Finally, the situation escalated to where I could not stand any more. It was going beyond just me, it started to impact my family. I knew I had had enough, and had to make one of the most difficult decisions I could at the time. It was time to end the relationship. Months after I was depressed and dissociated. Even with my great support system and great friends the anxiety became rooted in the back of my head. I didn't want to go to school. I developed an eating disorder. I constantly struggled with managing my emotions.

Eventually, it hit the point where my mom sat me down and said I should look into therapy. I questioned this decision for a while. Why would I talk to a stranger? Why would I open up to someone I don't even know? I went from July-December living through this dejected state. Somehow I did know that how I was living was not very fulfilling. At last I decided I was willing to give it a try.

Now, I'm so glad I did. I was able to work myself out of that depressed state of mind with guidance. I now think it genuinely saved my life.

Your child choosing therapy does not mean you are a failure as a parent. My mom has experience as a crisis intervention therapist at a high school, and it took seeking outside help for me to be able to begin healing. A third party to talk to made processing everything a lot easier. Therapy helped me view the situation through the eyes of someone who was not personally involved. I received advice and guidance I never would have thought of. I now believe going to therapy does not mean you are weak. It does not mean there is something wrong with you. Years later I still regularly check in with my therapist, even if there is not something negatively affecting my quality of life. I would recommend therapy to anyone who is interested in healing, or even just learning more about themselves. I'm so glad I finally listened to my mom's recommendation. It truly changed my life for the better and I still use the things I learned about myself and about mental health in my day-to-day life."

How Physical Health Affects Mental Health

Through my own journey with depression, I've come to deeply understand how our physical and mental health are closely linked. Regular exercise has become a crucial part of my routine, not just for the physical benefits or the boost in self-esteem, but as a vital strategy for managing my mental wellbeing. It's a clear example of how taking care of our bodies can positively impact our mental health. But it's not just about working out; I've noticed four key areas—sleep, eating habits, staying hydrated, and regular physical activity—that young adults really need to get a handle on. Addressing these areas can significantly improve both their physical and mental health, ideally before they venture out on their own.

Sleep is a big deal when it comes to mental health, and if you've ever been in the trenches of parenting a teenager or young adult, you know it's a common battleground. We'll dive into the tech versus sleep showdown later, but for now, let's focus on why sleep is so important. Basically, it boils down to two things: restoration and memory consolidation. When we snooze, our brains are doing some heavy lifting—clearing out the junk and making sense of the day's events. Skip out on sleep, and your brain's ability to process and remember things takes a hit. If you've ever pulled an all-nighter, you know exactly what I'm talking about. Sleep isn't just about recharging your brain or sorting through the day's memories; it plays a huge role in how we feel, too. When we miss out on sleep, we're not just groggy. We're grumpier, more stressed, and sitting ducks for depression. On the flip side, getting plenty of good-quality sleep is like emotional armor, making us better at handling life's ups and downs. Skimp on it, and you're likely to find your mood in the dumps, affecting not just how you feel, but also how well you complete tasks the following day.

Eating right is just as crucial as sleeping well when it comes to keeping our brains in top shape. While we won't get into the nitty-gritty of vitamins, minerals, and all that jazz, it's pretty clear that what we eat plays a big role in how our brain functions. A balanced diet keeps the brain healthy, sharpens our thinking, and can even keep mental health issues at bay. Sure, a healthy diet is a long game, but even short-term food choices, like a sugar rush or a caffeine spike, can mess with our moods and emotions. Speaking of caffeine, did you know it's globally the most addicted chemical on the planet? Not shocking for us coffee lovers, but it does make you think. It's not just caffeine affecting us either; our modern world is full of substances that can tweak our brain chemistry, from ADHD meds to THC. I'm not here to lecture on drug prevention, but it's a short step from recognizing how everything we ingest—from our morning coffee to whatever else—can impact our mental and physical health. Convincing our young adults to be mindful of what they consume is key to them taking control of their health, starting with their diet.

Sticking with the "chemistry" theme, H2O is like the unsung hero of our body's chemistry, playing a star role in how we feel and function. Growing up, the only hydration advice I got was to drink up to avoid leg cramps during sports. But diving a bit deeper into the science, it turns out that even being a little dehydrated can mess with our moods, making us feel anxious, cranky, and just plain tired. It doesn't stop there—our brain's ability to focus and store memories also takes a hit without enough water. On a happier note, staying well-hydrated can actually make us feel more content by dialing down stress's physical toll. Nowadays, I'm pretty mindful about how much water I drink, even keeping an eye on the color of my pee (yep, you read that right) as a quick hydration check. (Pro tip: You want your pee to be clear, not deep yellow, to know you're on the right track.) It's become my personal mission to stay hydrated, and I'm passing that wisdom on to my young adults because, let's face it, managing our water intake is a big deal.

Finally, exercise isn't just about getting in shape or hitting those fitness milestones; it's a game-changer for our mental health, too. Hitting the gym, going for a run, or just moving more, can seriously dial down the stress and anxiety levels. It's about those endorphins—the body's natural mood lifters and painkillers—giving us that famous "runner's high." Beyond the buzz, regular physical activity is a powerhouse for boosting self-esteem, improving how we feel about our bodies, and even getting the blood flowing better to our brain. Bottom line: making exercise a regular part of life is a big win for our mental wellbeing.

Using the WISE Method to Connect Physical and Mental Health

To bridge the gap between physical and mental health for our young adults, it all starts with their awareness and readiness to take action. This is where focusing on their **Willingness to Learn and Set a Goal** comes into play. Initiate the conversation with something like, "How about we chat about our daily routines, like how our diet and sleep influence our mood and energy levels. What do you think about setting some goals in this area?" As parents, our aim is to gauge if they grasp the connections between physical health and mental wellness.

Once our young adults show they're keen on making a change, it's time to see if they've put their plans into action. Spotting their **Initiate and Implement** phase can be as simple as noticing they're sticking to a good sleep routine, choosing healthier snacks, or getting into a workout groove. The **Sustained Practice** part is when they keep at it, tracking their wins in a journal or an app, and even pat themselves on the back for hitting those weekly targets. Sure, they might stumble now and then, but it's their dedication to stay on track that makes the difference.

Our young adults truly step into their own in managing their health and wellness when they reach the **Evaluate and Evolve** stage. This is when they actively tweak their routines, try out new exercises or nutritional plans, and aren't shy about consulting the pros for extra guidance. Seeing them making informed choices and adjustments are clear signals that they're well on their path to maintaining their physical and mental health independently.

Physical and Mental Health and the ADULT Method

Kicking off the ADULT approach, we start with a straightforward **Ask** to open the dialogue. It goes something like: "Lately, I've been thinking that staying physically active could play a big role in our overall mood and mental wellbeing. What's your take on that? Have you felt any different when you're up and about more, compared to when you're not?" This question sets the stage for a true conversation, encouraging them to share their experiences and views on the impact physical activity has on their mental health.

Shifting into the **Discussion and Dialogue** phase, you might say, "Hearing about your experiences is really interesting. Do you think certain exercises have a stronger positive impact on your mental state?" This exchange can uncover a lot. Maybe they're already on board with the **Willingness to Learn** and **Initiate and Implement** stages, yet sticking with these habits is where they stumble. Or it could turn out they've been in a routine for ages and now it's time for them to **Evaluate and Evolve** their approach. This part of the conversation is about exploring their thoughts and actions in a natural, engaging way, helping you understand where they're at without coming across as if you're issuing orders.

If we discover there's something we'd like to suggest they try, we could move to the "**U**" in the **ADULT** method, the **Up to You Suggestion**. "It sounds great what you've been doing. It's completely up to you, but have you considered trying ____ ? I think it would align with what you enjoy."

We next approach the **Lean In** or persuasion part of our **ADULT** strategy a bit differently. Here's the thing: we're nudging them towards making their own choices, gently suggesting paths they might take. You can say, "You know, I've found that squeezing in a walk or a quick exercise session really helps me focus and chill out. Ever thought about fitting in some regular activity that you'd enjoy?" This approach nudges without outright pushing, maintaining that parent-child dynamic where our "suggestions" often carry a bit more weight, hinting that we'd really like them to consider it. However, if we're genuinely concerned that their mental wellbeing could take a hit from neglecting sleep, nutrition, hydration, or exercise, then maybe it's time to **Lean In**. We're aiming for their independence, but there are moments when a stronger nudge towards healthier habits is necessary.

When our nudges and dialogues don't quite hit the mark, we can choose to tap into the expertise of a **Third Party** or **Trained Expert**. It's a good move when our young adults aren't reaping the mental health perks from their fitness grind, and we're like, "Hey, ever thought about getting some insights from a fitness trainer or a health counselor?" We, as parents, can open doors for them to explore professional advice, gently suggesting a path forward without pushing. This approach helps maintain their autonomy while ensuring they get the support they need to thrive mentally and physically. It's our way of saying, "There are folks who can tailor advice just for you. Interested?"

Sometimes, stepping into the "**T**" mode—connecting our young adults with a **Third Party** or **Trained Expert**—means we've also got to be a bit of a guide through the wilds of internet info. It's no secret: the web's a jungle of good, bad, and ugly advice. So, while our kids might be quick to Google their way through life's questions, we can play a crucial role in steering them in the right direction. It's doable to show them how to discern and pick out the best, most trustworthy sources among the online chaos.

Remember, hopping over to "**T**" is always on the table, no matter where you're at in the conversation. Back in the diaper days, we were the go-to for all the answers. Now, as they're getting savvy, it's on us to demonstrate the art of seeking out solid, expert advice.

Handling Stress: A Must-Learn for Thriving Young Adults

In today's whirlwind world, learning to manage stress is like holding the golden ticket to wellbeing. Young adults who are riding the rollercoaster of change need this skill more than ever. It's not enough to bounce back; They should learn to spot when stress and anxiety are sneaking up on them. They've got a whole lineup of challenges waiting, so let's get them ready. We'll start with stress-spotting 101, then dive into how to dial it back.

First off, let's talk about spotting stress and anxiety. When you start feeling more scared, worried, or down than usual, and it doesn't quite match up with what's going on externally, that's a hint that you might be dealing with anxiety. For younger folks, this can show up as trouble focusing, not doing as well at work or school, or even starting to dodge people and places they used to be comfortable with. If they're putting off stuff they need to do or stepping back from fun activities without a clear reason, that's another signal. It's like their usual personality has done a 180, and if there's no other way to pin it down, stress or anxiety could be the troublemaker here.

Stress and anxiety can mess with your actions and your body. Feeling super irritable, changing up how much you eat or sleep, or pulling away from your friends and family? Those could be signs. It might not all just take place in your head – we're talking stomach pains, feeling wiped out all the time, or persistent or frequent headaches.

What we would like is to equip our young adults with some solid strategies to tackle stress and anxiety. Mindfulness practices might be the answer, like attending a yoga class or focusing on their breath to calm the mind. Meditation or other cool-down techniques can also be a big help. Don't write off the basics. Getting enough sleep, eating well, and reducing caffeine and sugar intake can make a huge difference in managing stress. Throwing some exercise into the mix, even something as simple as a daily walk, can do wonders too. We've talked about how nailing these healthy habits isn't just good for the body; it's key to knocking down stress, cutting through anxiety, and dodging the depression bullet.

Another solid move against stress and anxiety? Simply talking it out with friends, family, or a counselor. Handling our emotions isn't something we're born knowing how to do – it's a skill we've got to pick up along the way. If chatting with a counselor is what's needed, we should encourage our kids to give it a shot. We in the U.S. have made some strides in casting off the mental health stigma, but we've still got a ways to go. Keeping an open mind about getting help from pros or outside sources can make all the difference.

What we definitely don't want is for our young adults to start relying on substances to get through the highs and lows of life. It's pretty clear that using stuff that messes with your mood or mind can actually change how your brain works over time. The last thing we want is for our kid to feel like they need alcohol, THC, or any stimulants or depressants just to shake off a bad mood. However, this kind of temptation is everywhere for young adults. Chances are, they've got friends who think this is an easy out. While I can't highlight every single way parents can combat drug use here, know this: your role is huge in keeping them clear of addiction. Open, honest chats without judgment can do wonders. Listen about where they're coming from and if they're leaning on substances, understand why. Is there something else going on that they're trying to deal with? You can chat about the real risks of substance abuse and propose healthier ways to handle stress. Remember, there's expert help available everywhere for both the person dealing with substance use and even for their loved ones. Don't let stigma hold your kids back from seeking support. Being proactive is far better than regretting not speaking up when self-medicating with substances becomes a habit.

"Reframing" is also an interesting concept that helps flip the script on stress and anxiety. Start by addressing the gloomy thoughts that might drag your kid down. Then, encourage your child to give the thoughts a good reality check– are they really the truth, or just some stories they've told themselves. Questioning these thoughts can seriously dial down the worry. Sure, some stuff in life just stinks – like bombing a big game or going through a tough breakup. But even then, there's a silver lining if you look for what you can learn, rather than stewing in negativity. Hunting for the positive spin helps us break free from that doom-loop. It takes a bit of practice, but tackling those negative thought patterns head-on can be a game-changer for mental peace. If this is new for you, it's worth diving into some solid resources for you and your young adult to get the hang of it all. Finding a feeling of control and self-soothing is totally doable.

The WISE Goals for Dealing with Stress and Anxiety

Tackling stress with the **WISE** approach is pretty much a no-brainer. Let's kick it off with **Willingness to Learn and Set a Goal**. Do our young folks get why it's key to spot stress signals and have a plan in place to deal with them? They need to know stress is just part of life, and it's how you handle it that counts. Have they caught on to the stress signs we've talked about? And are they considering any stress relief strategies? Managing stress isn't just nice; it's crucial for not letting stress sabotage our day-to-day lives.

Moving on to **Initiate and Implement**, are they actually putting any stress-busting moves into action? Maybe they're jotting down how they're feeling each day, or giving deep breathing or meditation a try. If they've started tackling their stress, are they keeping at it with **Sustained Practice**? Making these techniques a regular thing can increase their effectiveness and make handling stress easier long-term. If all is going well, are they **Evaluating and Evolving**? They can continue getting more efficient at managing stress and being open to seeking help when it gets tough. Maybe they even share their wisdom with friends. Nailing these steps isn't just about fighting stress; it's a roadmap toward personal growth, getting to know themselves better, and learning how to keep calm, no matter what life throws their way.

Applying the ADULT Method about Stress and Anxiety

Diving into the **ADULT** method, we start with **Ask**. Check in with your young adult: "Do you catch yourself feeling super stressed? What tips you off that stress is creeping in?" We can start the initial conversation and encourage them to reflect on their emotions. These interactions also help them understand that you want to validate how they feel. This shows them that you, as their parent, want to create a safe place for them to express and examine their emotions. **Dialogue** is a chance to get a deeper sense of where they stand with the **WISE** goals. Perhaps dig a bit more: "Tried any cool ways to dial down the stress? Spotted what usually kicks off your stress?" This stage is all about chatting through their experiences, figuring out if they've started tackling stress head-on, and what specifics set it off. This step is a mix of playing detective and supporter, helping them navigate through recognizing and managing their stress.

The **Up to You Suggestion** is for gently dropping in your own two cents. Maybe try "Hey, I've heard about some neat tricks like mindfulness or getting moving that could really take the edge off stress. Totally your call if you want to give them a whirl." Maybe add: "Interested in chatting about how these could work for you?" It's a soft nudge, offering options without pushing. This step is for suggesting, not insisting. Keep the door open for them to explore stress-busting techniques that might catch their eye.

When hitting the **Lean In** phase, it's clear that maybe our young adult needs a bit more from us to tackle stress and anxiety. This is where you might try suggesting something you've tried like, "I've found yoga or journaling is a game-changer in keeping stress at bay. What do you think about trying them out?" We can now feel comfortable with offering extra guidance, based on what we've learned could help. If you're feeling out of your depth, that's where a **Third Party** or **Trained Expert** comes in. It's crucial we move past any hang-ups about seeking professional advice. The real deal is getting our children the support they need, which should far outweigh any concerns about stigma. Seeing a counselor or getting expert advice isn't a sign of failure; it's about doing what's best. Especially knowing how deep and dark it can get for some young folks, where they feel cornered by their thoughts, it's a no-brainer: skip the stigma, go for the support.

Going back to where we kicked things off, the whole journey

begins with getting savvy about the signs of stress, anxiety, depression, and fear. If our kids are going to stand on their own two feet, understanding this stuff is non-negotiable. More than anything, they should grasp the different cues as to when they're capable of tackling stress and anxiety solo and when it's time to wave in some backup. Make sure you're not the wall blocking them from seeking the help they might need. Show them enough love, support, and acceptance to equip them for success in this tricky, often taboo, territory. You're capable of giving them the tools and the green light to face these challenges head-on, showing them when and how to ask for help.

An Erick Story: There's Always Something New

"I'd like to say this happens only occasionally, but I'm pretty sure it happens all of the time. Each generation of parents has to confront a new technology that affects their children in a way their own parents never had to deal with. For example, most of today's parents have probably done some video gaming. They've probably had cell phones most of their lives. Both of those were new technologies when we were raising our kids. We had to make brand new decisions on when our kids would have access to each (tweens and teens for our kids.) I remember many parents making different decisions than we did, so there were no 'best practices' in our neighborhood. We were all making it up as we went along.

Another of those new technologies is vaping. It came long just as my kids were entering college. I never thought I'd have to worry about my kids smoking and/or having a nicotine addiction. I had lived through watching every member of my family quit, including myself. Smoking amongst teens had seemed to be declining for years.

But then one day my son came home from college and he was vaping. I immediately thought it was THC (marijuana) and 'lost my shit.' But he explained it was only nicotine so what could I say? It certainly wasn't illegal.

But a few months later my son reported he was getting sick a lot. A chest cold is what he told us. It took a few more months before we finally convinced him to see a doctor. Turns out he was using the cheaper vape pens and had developed a lung infection because of the chemicals they were using in the cartridges. I guess he had what some have called a mild version of 'popcorn lung.'

This was bad, I figured. In his middle twenties and now he has a lung problem. But I guess the doctor explained to him it was primarily because he was using the cheaper vapes. In the end, he didn't stop vaping. He upgraded and he hasn't reported to us recently any lung issues.

But I'm still concerned. I think if this had been around when he lived at home we could have had more impact on this topic. It certainly can't be good to put anything in your lungs that might even slightly clog them up. And, of course, nicotine addiction is a terrible thing that is very hard to quit. (I know. Took me years and six 'quits' to finally quit.) But all I can do now is try to get around to the conversation. Try an 'Ask' and 'Dialogue' and see where it goes.

There will always be new technologies that we're going to be worried about. That's why teaching them how to be healthy is more important than telling them what they can or cannot do. It's the old 'teach a man to fish' problem. Better to know 'why' and 'how' than to simply know 'what.'"

CHAPTER 5 - SOCIAL WELLBEING AND NAVIGATING RELATIONSHIPS

Research by Rath and Harter highlights that thriving in life is deeply connected to high social wellbeing, emphasizing the crucial role of strong, quality relationships. It's a no-brainer that lacking meaningful connections is pretty much the opposite of living your best life, a theme we've seen play out in countless movies. This chapter dives into the complex factors influencing our interactions with others, including the variety of friendships and acquaintances we might have, the impact of our personalities on these relationships, the importance of emotional intelligence, and the undeniable influence of digital media on our social lives. Let's unpack how understanding these elements can enhance our young adults' ability to navigate and enrich their social world.

Navigating All of the Different Types of Relationships

First up, let's tackle the idea that not everyone in our lives needs the "best friend" label. Picture our varying relationships like a set of concentric circles, with "friends of friends" forming the outermost ring. There are some people we know and are connected to but in a very loose way. It's key for our young adults to grasp that their buddies also have their own networks.

These outer-circle connections might not be like us in terms of interests or personalities, yet they're kind of pre-approved by the people we know. This concept of "loose ties" can expand our children's social worlds, introducing them to new ideas and opportunities. Remember, though, that these outer-ring pals are beyond our control and can shake up the usual social vibe, making interactions a bit of a mixed bag. We want our child to expand their social network and not be socially insulated by just a few friends. So, hey, variety is the spice of life, right? Fortunately, over the years, your young adult will cross paths with thousands of these acquaintances, each one adding a unique flavor to their social mix.

There are many different groups we acquire. For example, there are those pals we link up with through hobbies or extracurriculars. Think about the folks you bump into at your weekly soccer game or the regulars at your favorite coffee joint. These connections, sparked by shared interests or activities, might not always evolve into BFF-status relationships for your kid, but they're valuable nonetheless. Over time, some might become closer to them, joining their inner circle, while others remain in the realm of hobby buddies. And that's perfectly fine and normal. These activity-based friendships add richness and diversity to our social lives, reminding us that not every friendship has to fit the same mold to be meaningful.

There is also the "casual acquaintance" category—those folks we're happy to chat with when we bump into them but wouldn't necessarily schedule a hangout with. This group can offer a wide array of perspectives and experiences, though the interactions may tend to skim the surface, lacking the depth and emotional connection of closer friendships. Within this category, there's a niche for work or school friends. These are the people we share significant amounts of time with due to shared tasks or goals, yet they don't make it into our innermost circle.

However, we want to help our young adult understand that navigating these "forced" relationships can sometimes stir up drama or conflict, especially if there is competition or boundary issues at play. Keeping these relationships friendly, despite the challenges, is something many of us learn to manage over time. It's not uncommon for work or school friends to remain in this steady state for years—never getting much closer, but also not drifting apart. Discussing this balance will showcase to your young adult that they need the ability to maintain a broad spectrum of friendships, understanding that each has its place and value in the tapestry of their social lives.

In the innermost circle, we find our closest friends—the ones we chat with often and lean on during tough times. These are the relationships that take time and effort to build, yet they form the cornerstone of our social support system, characterized by deep trust and mutual understanding. The intensity of these connections, however, means that conflicts can be particularly painful, and there's a risk of dependency, where one person might lean too heavily on the other for their social and emotional needs. Despite these challenges, the value of having such close friendships can't be overstated. Beyond family, these are the bonds we truly hope our young adults will cultivate and maintain throughout their lives. The presence of best friends not only enriches our daily experiences, but also provides a sense of belonging and emotional security that's essential for personal growth and happiness. Investing in relationships nurtures wellbeing and offers our young adults a safe space to be their true selves.

At the heart of our social connections lie intimate relationships, the deepest and most profound bonds we form. Whether it's a series of significant others over the years, or a lifelong partnership that starts as high school sweethearts, navigating these waters is complex and challenging. As parents of young adults, we're often drawn into discussions about these relationships, though, interestingly, these talks rarely center on the physical aspects. While the dynamics of intimacy might vary from one family to another, with some parents choosing to discuss all facets, it seems today's youth often gain knowledge about the physical intimacy aspect from sources outside the home. The essence of the conversations at home often focus more on the emotional and psychological components of forming and maintaining deep, intimate connections. I believe these conversations should highlight the importance of understanding, respect, and communication as foundational elements of any significant relationship. As we guide our young adults through the maze of intimate relationships, our role is to support them in learning how to build partnerships based on mutual respect, love, and shared values, preparing them for the complexities and joys of the deepest human connections.

Guiding Through Relationship Challenges

When it comes to intimate relationships, sometimes our talks revolve around moments of tension and conflict, rather than the birds and the bees. Two major hurdles that many couples need to navigate are communication issues and balancing independence with togetherness. First off, mastering the art of open, honest, and respectful dialogue with a partner is crucial. It's something we, as parents, can really help our young adults with. We can encourage them to express their feelings, listen actively, and tackle problems together, rather than letting them simmer. The second biggie is navigating the tightrope walk between being your own person and being part of a duo. It should be a goal to find that sweet spot where you support each other's individual dreams and aspirations, while building a shared life together. This dance of managing dependence is tricky, especially when you're pretty much living in each other's pockets as life partners and, possibly, roommates. There's a lot we can do to prepare our kids for these relationship realities. Teaching them to communicate effectively and maintain their sense of self within a partnership are invaluable lessons that can help them forge stronger, healthier relationships.

It's no secret that the cornerstone of any lasting intimate relationship is solid communication, a theme as prevalent in therapy sessions as it is in pop culture. The skills involved—active listening, sharing thoughts and feelings openly, and responding without passing judgment—are crucial, yet challenging to master. It's essential to recognize that these abilities aren't innate; they're developed through a mix of trial and error and, ideally, through direct teaching and observation. As parents, we have a prime opportunity to model effective communication for our kids and young adults. They're always watching, learning from how we handle tough talks and bounce back from disagreements. By demonstrating healthy communication habits, including how to engage in difficult conversations and resolve conflict, we provide them with a live playbook to reference in their own relationships. This emphasis on communication isn't just theoretical; it's a continuous personal journey. Actively working on enhancing communication skills is a lifelong commitment.

The journey of intertwining lives in an intimate partnership is complex. Contrary to the fairy-tale narrative of "happily ever after," the reality involves handling the delicate balance between independence and interdependence—a task that's crucial for the health of any relationship. Encouraging personal passions, maintaining friendships outside the relationship, and pursuing individual goals are key to personal fulfillment and safeguarding against codependency. However, the dance between doing things together and apart isn't guided by any set rules or equations. It's a dynamic process, sensitive to the unique context of the relationship and the individuals within it. Imagine a pendulum swinging—sometimes it might lean too much towards one person's needs or too far away from togetherness. As parents, we can hope to gently guide it back towards equilibrium using the "WISE ADULT" method, though ideally, our young adults will learn to self-regulate this balance. While the complexities of friendships and intimate relationships could fill volumes beyond what's covered here, it's crucial to explore these dynamics thoughtfully. Before we turn to a new topic, let's ensure we've considered how the "WISE ADULT" method applies, encouraging our young adults to navigate these waters with wisdom and self-awareness. For a deeper dive into these essential life skills, seeking out additional resources is highly recommended.

Applying WISE to Friendships and Relationships

The journey to understanding and nurturing relationships starts with a **Willingness to Learn and Set a Goal**. Our young adults need to grasp the essence of fostering both intimate and casual connections with effort, understanding, and respect. Aiming to sharpen their communication skills and establish healthy boundaries is paramount. Moving to **Initiate and Implement**, this is where we can ensure they're putting these goals into action. This means they're practicing engaged listening and being proactive in their interactions, including setting and honoring boundaries.

The **Sustained Practice** phase is where consistency comes into play. Regularly touching base with friends and partners to ensure mutual satisfaction in the relationship is a sign of their commitment to maintaining healthy connections. Reaching **Evaluate and Evolve** involves self-reflection on their relationships. Are their needs being met? Are they considering the needs of others? This is where they should address any issues, deepen certain bonds, and possibly redefine or end others based on these reflections.

When our young adults navigate these stages independently, adjusting their relationships as needed, while prioritizing mutual respect and fulfillment, it's clear evidence of their maturity and our success in guiding them. This approach not only sets them up for healthier existing relationships, but also lays the groundwork for future connections.

Inquiring with the ADULT Method

The ADULT method kicks off with **Ask**. Asking "Have you ever considered the variety of friendships in your life? What qualities do you treasure most in these relationships?" lays the foundation for exploring connections. This initial question naturally segues into **Discussion and Dialogue**, where we focus on their experiences of feeling supported or, conversely, unsupported by friends. Questions like, "What made that support feel meaningful? Is there something more you're seeking in these friendships, or something your friends might be seeking from you?" help uncover nuances in their relationships. By engaging in these conversations, we gain insight into our young adult's perceptions and expectations of their friendships, but also guide them in reflecting on the importance of mutual support, understanding, and respect in their interactions. This process aids their personal growth and strengthens their ability to build and maintain fulfilling relationships.

By offering **Up to You Suggestions**, we propose potential actions without pressure. Suggesting, "It might be worth having a chat to explore both your and your friend's feelings," provides them with a new perspective, while emphasizing the choice is theirs. This approach encourages autonomy in decision-making regarding their relationships. When necessary, **Lean In** emphasizes the importance of effective communication for trust and support within any relationship. Advising, "Communication can be challenging, but it's crucial for a healthy relationship. Maybe give that conversation another shot" nudges them towards positive action, highlighting the value of persistence in addressing relationship issues. If the situation proves too complex, turning to a **Third Party** or **Trained Expert** becomes a valuable step. Suggesting, "If this relationship issue is causing significant stress, talking to a counselor might provide some clarity," opens the door to professional guidance, reinforcing the idea that seeking help is a smart and constructive choice.

Applying the ADULT method in this way assists young adults in navigating the complexities of their relationships, and instills critical life skills like effective communication, decision-making, and when to seek external support.

Preparing for Life's Social Seas

In the vast "wild" of the real world, our role isn't to micromanage our child's social circle. We are responsible for equipping them with the skills and insights needed to weather the sometimes turbulent waters of relationships. We understand that life's social dynamics can be unpredictable, filled with both rewarding connections and challenging encounters. The "WISE ADULT" method check-in offers us a structured approach to bolster their social navigational tools if necessary. This method encompasses recognizing the value of diverse relationships, initiating and maintaining healthy interactions, and evolving personal approaches to better manage and enrich these connections. Our ultimate goal is to ensure they're well-prepared for the journey ahead, capable of forming meaningful relationships, are discerning in their choice of companions, and resilient in the face of social challenges. By applying the "WISE ADULT" method, we guide them towards becoming self-reliant individuals. We want to raise individuals who are ready to thrive within the world's social "wild," armed with the wisdom and adaptability to navigate life's choppy waters with grace and confidence.

An Erick Story: Teenagers Can Be Cruel, Especially To Each Other

"When my daughter hit high school she started to pull away from me. That was truly painful. She was the one who was always the

happiest to see me. The one who jumped on me from the couch and just seemed to love being in my arms. When she started to separate and have conversations with my wife that I was no longer a part of, everyone told me it was just a phase. She'd reconnect with me some day. Just be patient.

First, I can tell you they were right. We've had a great relationship for several years. But I still regret that I wasn't there to help her during some trying teenage years. One incident in particular sticks out to me. There was another girl she used to hang out with and I thought they were best friends. But that was sometimes hard to figure out since my daughter easily moved between social groups. One day I learned that this particular girl had really turned on my daughter. It really devastated my daughter and, I believe, shook her confidence to the core. To have someone you trust make such a 180 on you I know was really hard. I think it contributed to her getting into a bad romantic relationship shortly afterward.

I'm grateful my wife had an open line of communication with her when I didn't. And that's my first piece of advice. Try to have one of the parents keep an open line of communication. But more importantly, try to build up your teenager's confidence when their social life takes a dramatic turn for the worse. I wish that I could have told my daughter back then that it was all going to turn out all right. That she was a great person and it was her friend's loss to shut her out like that. I wish I could have just sat down on the couch and let her cry it all out. Because sometimes that's all you need to do. Not solve it. Just be there and let them cry it all out.

If there is a happy ending to this story it is that my daughter seems to have a bunch of close friends in her life now. She lives on the other side of the country but we know she can easily call 20 friends if she needs to. And her social life is as busy as anyone's we know. I don't know if she's simply gotten better at picking friends, or if it was just a phase all teenagers, particularly girls, have to go through - discovering how cruel other teenagers can be. But she's fine. Sometimes you don't have the solution. They learn as they grow."

Understanding Personality in Social

Dynamics: The Importance of Self-Knowledge

Recognizing our own personality traits is crucial for smoothly navigating our social circles. Whether you're the life of the party or a homebody, a nature enthusiast or someone who prefers the indoors, understanding these aspects of yourself is important. It can significantly enhance our interactions and friendships. With countless personality assessments available, from those aimed at career guidance to personal development, diving into these resources can offer valuable insights. For a more serious exploration into personality analysis, I recommend opting for scientifically-backed surveys like those from "Psychology Today", as opposed to the more casual, entertainment-focused quizzes.

For this section, I'll concentrate on just three aspects of personality that have a direct impact on our social relationships. These include our communication style, our approach to conflict resolution, and our social energy.

Getting a handle on how we chat and connect with folks is a big deal for making our social life run smoothly. Some of us are chatty, while others are all ears. This whole talk-listening thing might link up with being an introvert or an extrovert, but that's just one piece of the puzzle in figuring out our chat style.

Ever noticed whether you're a storyteller who goes on and on, or someone who gets straight to the point? Or maybe you're wondering if your jokes hit the mark or kinda flop. And what about talking politics—are you all in, or is that a no-go zone for you? Everyone's got their unique way of talking and listening, and that's cool. But knowing your style and how it jives (or doesn't) with the folks you hang out with can make a world of difference. If you're on the quiet side, maybe it's time to participate in more chats. On the other hand, if you're usually holding the mic, learning when to step back can be a good chance for you to take in what's happening around you and just experience the moment. It's also about figuring out what kinds of conversation styles click with you when you're with others. Getting a fix on your own chat habits and what you dig in conversations can seriously up your friendship game. For young adults especially, getting this right means making every chat, hangout, or heart-to-heart that much better.

It's also key for our young adults to get the scoop on how they naturally deal with disagreements. Some folks are all about dodging conflict, while others tackle it head-on. It's crucial to figure out if sometimes your child needs to switch up their approach. The way we handle clashes plays a big part in who we jive with and why. It's also important to find out what kind of social scene gets us excited. Some people are all in for big parties, love meeting new folks, and are pretty much the life of the party. Many other people have more quiet dispositions, enjoy deeper conversation, and are interested in really getting to know someone one-on-one. How we like to mingle and hang out guides us in picking our go-to spots and people. I tend to steer clear of loud, wild places filled with people I don't know. Knowing that helps me brace for the occasions when I will find myself in a loud environment, but also helps me enjoy the quieter conversations I seek out. Figuring out your social preferences while you are growing up often means checking out a mix of scenes, and that's totally cool. We want our young adults to try different settings and discover what and who makes them comfortable and happy.

Reflecting on Social Interactions with the WISE Method

Tackling the "W" or **Willingness to Learn** in our WISE goals is all about peeling back the layers on how our young adults see their way of chatting it up, squaring off in disagreements, and what kind of hangouts get them excited. It's a big puzzle—knowing if they're tuned into the energy their personality brings to the party and how that plays out in the social arena. Are they keen on getting a grip on their unique quirks and using that intel to shape their social world? It's good to nudge our kids to think on their feet, take a hard look at their social habits, and see if there's room for a little tweaking. This step isn't just about them knowing themselves better, but also about being proactive in making their social life a better fit for them.

When our young adults hit the "I" for **Implement**, they're doing the work, adjusting how they mingle based on their self-discovery. Whether it's big shifts or not, they're enhancing their social game. By the time they reach **Sustained Practice**, they'll hopefully have a rhythm going where they size up social scenes and pick what interaction types agree with their likes and needs, all while keeping an eye on how others roll. Say they're more of the quiet type who digs deep talks—they're actively hunting for spots where those meaningful exchanges happen. Now, if they're in the **Evaluate and Evolve** stage, they're doing some reflection post-hangout. They're thinking about ironing out any kinks or missteps in their social dances. And as the social landscape shifts, they can adjust their approach to keep their social life active, without it being exhausting.

If our young adult is using their deep dive into their personality to build and nurture relationships that feel right, we've aced our role. Let them find their social sweet spot, where their interactions are both fulfilling for them and respectful of the diverse social styles around them.

Engaging with the ADULT Method

Kicking off with **Ask**, we honor their journey to self-discovery, not jumping the gun to lecture mode. We might toss out, "What sort of interactions pump you up or wear you out?" or "How'd you feel about the way you and your buddy worked through that recent spat?" It's smart to start that initial conversation with just being willing to listen and learn about where they are with understanding themselves and their social worlds.

In **Discussion and Dialogue,** we get a little deeper, still keeping it chill and open-ended. Questions like, "Are you the one doing most of the talking, or are you lending an ear more?" or "What's your take on what sparked that argument, and how'd you go about sorting it out?" help us get a sense of how they see their role in their relationships and conflicts. When it's time to possibly drop some wisdom with an **Up to You Suggestion**, we start with a gentle, "It's your call, but exploring different ways to handle disagreements could be helpful. Wanna pick that apart together?" It's about suggesting without pushing, guiding them to consider expanding their toolkit for dealing with clashes. If we sense they need more direction, we **Lean In** with something like, "You've mentioned loving deep talks, yet you're hitting up these super loud parties a lot. What's up with that? Can we unpack it a bit?" Sometimes they'll need some encouragement to reflect on their choices and decide whether those align with their preferences. If the waves seem too choppy for just us to navigate, suggesting a **Third Party** or **Trained Expert** might be the next step. It's about opening the door to professional insights, making sure they know it's okay to seek help when they're in over their heads.

Applying the ADULT method here is aimed toward guiding our young adults through the maze of social interactions and conflicts. We should respect their autonomy, while being ready to support, suggest, and sometimes steer them towards additional resources.

The journey of navigating social relationships involves learning on the go and making room for the occasional slip-up. Our young adults, just like us, are going to stumble socially now and then. The real deal? We're helping them pursue growth. What we're really aiming for is to plant the idea deep in their hearts that having social relationships plays a large role in their happiness. It's not enough to just bounce back from those social stumbles, but they should understand that building and maintaining meaningful connections is key to a life well-lived, brimming with wellbeing. Encouraging our young adults to see each misstep as a stepping stone, rather than a setback, fosters resilience and an optimistic outlook. This perspective prepares them for the complex world of adult relationships and highlights the joy and fulfillment that come from deep, authentic connections.

EQ, Assertiveness, and Boundaries

Diving into the heart of what makes our social interactions tick, there's something called "emotional intelligence". It's sometimes referred to as EQ for "Emotional Quotient" reminiscent of "IQ" for "Intelligence Quotient". The EQ skill set helps us get savvy with our own emotions, pick up on how others are feeling, and handle both with finesse. With a strong EQ, we're better thinkers, communicators, and friends, leveling up our ability to connect and vibe with people around us. I recommend taking a deeper look at EQ with Daniel Goleman's groundbreaking read, "Emotional Intelligence." It's a treasure trove of insights that I recommend if you're keen on mastering the art of being emotional savvy.

I consider having a high EQ like holding a key to overall wellbeing. It's not just about feeling good mentally and physically; it's also a big player in dialing down anxiety and keeping the blues at bay. When your EQ is off the charts, it means you've got this superpower to really get where people are coming from emotionally, paving the way for solid, supportive connections. You can read the room, navigate the day-to-day social dance with ease, and level up your chat game. Beyond just making you socially adept, it sharpens your decision-making skills and fuels your personal growth journey, making you a well-rounded individual ready to take on the world.

Let's add a specific kind of skill I call "assertiveness." Picture laying your cards on the table—your beliefs, needs, opinions, and rights—without stepping on anyone else's toes, but also not letting yours get trampled on. There's a fine line between sticking up for yourself and keeping that empathy and understanding for others in check. It's a skill, which means young adults can improve it with a bit of practice and some solid guidance. Mastering assertiveness is about unlocking the ability to set healthy boundaries, saving heaps of time, energy, and protecting your emotional peace. It's being cool with saying "no" when you've got to, and tackling conflicts without turning everything into a drama fest. Getting assertive is a major confidence booster, reminding young adults they're worth listening to and have every right to stand their ground. While it's a win for their future career, it's also a game-changer right now, keeping stress, anger, and frustration from piling up. If there's one thing pushed in any leadership workshop for the younger crowd, it's getting assertive. It's a big deal.

Nailing assertiveness isn't just about the big showdowns, however. Sometimes, it's as simple as swapping a "you" for an "I" to keep things relaxed and avoid pointing fingers. Saying "I feel upset when I'm interrupted because it seems like my thoughts don't matter" sounds way less combative than "you always cut me off." It's possible to find a sweet spot between not saying enough and saying way too much. It's finding the right words at the right time, using all that emotional savvy we've been talking about. But here's the thing: without someone showing you the ropes, a lot of us end up learning by just winging it and watching how the folks around us, like our parents, handle their relationships. That's why it's important to guide our young adults on how to speak their mind clearly and kindly, because being a pro at assertive chat is a major leg up in work life and just about every other situation they'll find themselves in.

The WISE Method with Emotional Intelligence

We're all about watching our young adults level up through

those WISE goals as they cruise into the future. Like, are they aware of the whole emotional intelligence skill set and the art of assertive chatting? Are they **Willing to Learn** skills for those tricky, heavy talks? Are they actually rolling up their sleeves to change how they approach conflict, **Initiating** more "I feel this way" instead of "you make me feel" lines? Are they getting a handle on their emotions instead of letting their emotions handle them? You can help them discover if they're ready to start making some real changes to how they communicate and connect.

Are they hitting their stride with **Sustained Practice**, really getting into the groove of things by sticking with their new communication habits? For example, are they jotting down their thoughts in a daily journal or bouncing ideas off pals or mentors to get a fresh perspective? What about the **Evaluate and Evolve** stage? Are they taking a step back to really check out how far they've come with their emotional intelligence? Down the line, when they're flying solo, they're going to bump into situations where their EQ and ability to stand their ground with grace are going to be key. They need to be in tune with their progress, understand what's working, what's not, and be ready to adapt and grow as they face the wide world of relationships ahead.

Utilizing the ADULT Method

Kicking off with the ADULT strategy, we start with a simple **Ask**: "Hey, got a sec to chat about that fight you had?" This opener should lead into deeper **Dialogue**, where we can dive into the nitty-gritty: "Do you think your strategy worked, or is there something you might tweak next time?" It's great if they're thinking critically about their own experiences, assessing their effectiveness, and considering adjustments for future interactions.

Moving through the ADULT method, there comes a time for an **Up to You Suggestion**. "Hey, it's up to you, but do you want me to share something I did in a similar situation?" If it feels like we need to **Lean In** with a bit of assertiveness of our own, we can try: "Getting the hang of this isn't easy. Why don't you try writing down what you might try to do differently next time?" We should be nudging them towards recognizing the big-picture value of these skills while respecting that we want them to handle these situations in the future.

There's always the option to bring in a **Third Party**. We might say, "If you're feeling like this is a tough area for you, what about chatting with someone who's a pro in communication skills? They could offer some deeper insights that might click." You have the power to open the door to expert advice, making sure they know it's okay to seek out more help when they're aiming to level up their emotional and conversational skills.

Getting a handle on emotional intelligence and assertiveness is crucial for laying out needs and boundaries without tossing respect or empathy out the window. It's the secret to smoothing over conflicts, building trust, and keeping relationships on an even keel. Making sure our young adult is geared up for the big, wide world involves equipping them with these social superpowers they'll need to navigate the twists and turns of today's social landscape. It is totally possible to prepare them to handle whatever comes their way with grace, understanding, and a solid sense of self.

Digital Wellbeing and Social Media

The game has changed since back in the day, especially with everyone glued to their screens now. Our young folks are practically born with the internet as an extra limb and it's reshaping the social environment and connections in ways we're just starting to wrap our heads around. Before we tumble down the "everything was better back then" rabbit hole, there's a silver lining here. There are a bunch of ways being dialed in 24/7 and social media could be giving our young adults' social lives a boost. Let's take a moment to talk about the upsides of this digital era for relationships and connections.

First off, our kids are smashing the geography game when it comes to maintaining distance friendships way more than we ever could have. They're keeping friendships alive with folks from their high school and college years in ways that would've blown our minds back in the day. Thanks to the digital world at their fingertips, they're able to keep these friendships thriving, no matter how many miles or years stand between them. They are not just making new pals online; these real-life bonds can now more than ever be prevented from fading away just because life's path takes them to different places.

Then there's the whole new community social media can bring to the table for our kids. They have a global village in their pocket. This can help them find their tribe. The people who get them on a level we could only dream of as kids. Whether it's hobbies, hurdles, or life stories, they're never more than a few taps away from someone who shares their passions or pains. Talk about stepping up—some of these young people are even taking social platforms and turning them into megaphones for change. They're diving into activism, tossing their weight behind causes, and making waves in ways that would've felt far out of reach when we were their age. They're using the internet to find their voices and join bigger conversations and movements, something truly remarkable to see.

It's not all smooth sailing, though. Being plugged in 24/7 comes with its own set of hurdles. There's the trap of sinking too much time into scrolling through feeds, which can pull our kids away from face-to-face moments that count. This can lead them to feeling lonely or left out. They're bombarded with polished snapshots of others' lives, starting a game of comparison that nobody wins. This has the potential to drag down their self-worth and, in some cases, lead to depression. Let's not gloss over the whole privacy thing—the line between public and private is blurrier than ever, with personal details sometimes just a click away. So, what's the game plan? How do we guide our young adults to foster genuine, supportive connections in a world we're still learning to navigate right alongside them? I think we can help them focus on finding that balance, help them discern meaningful interactions from the noise, and encourage them to cultivate relationships that are rooted in real, shared experiences.

Absolutely the first step is amping up their digital smarts. Young adults need to know the lowdown on what's okay and what's risky. It's also about them taking a hard look at how they're jumping into the social media pool—like paying attention to how much time they spend scrolling. Can they draw the line when it comes to how much of their life they share and when it's time to just log off? It's crucial they find that sweet spot between living online and living it up in the real world. Having real talks about the good, the bad, and the ugly of social media and screen time is key. We want them to learn to guide themselves through their digital world wisely, keeping their wellbeing in check while taking advantage of all of the positives.

Sometimes, the best move is to get some insight from outside sources. While it's never a bad thing to look on the bright side, it's eye-opening to see the gaps in what our kids know about the digital world. I advise being on the ball, but not hitting the panic button. Every generation has its share of game-changing tech and cultural shifts, and we've all managed to find our way. This next generation will be no different. Our real mission is to arm them with the know-how they need to stand on their own two feet in a digital age that's full of social interactions, from the fleeting to the foundational.

Applying the WISE and ADULT Methods

Leveraging the WISE method, we're on a mission to ensure our young adults tackle the digital realm with a sense of responsibility and a knack for reaping its benefits. Are they **Willing to Learn** the ropes, especially in understanding how social media might be messing with their mental health, or affecting the dynamics of their real-world friendships? Are they setting goals for a more balanced online presence and carving out offline moments? Once they have their goals lined up, are they jumping into **Initiate and Implement** mode, tweaking those app privacy settings to keep their digital footprint in check? Later we're looking for **Sustained Practice** – are their online habits consistently reflecting their commitment to personal wellbeing? Recognizing the need for balance might mean getting comfy with new digital tools or strategies. When it's time to **Evaluate** and reflect, are they **Evolving** their approach, maybe by embracing digital detox days? Steering our young adults to be WISE is the blueprint for ensuring they cultivate a wholesome relationship with social media and tech. Living in the digital era doesn't change the timeless truth: thriving in life is deeply intertwined with nurturing solid social bonds.

Trying the ADULT strategy, we start with a simple, yet empowering **Ask** to show we respect their autonomy. We might toss out, "How's the social media scene treating you? Notice any shifts in your moods, or how your day pans out because of it?" Then, we pause and really listen. They might have this whole digital balancing act figured out, or maybe there's a chance to peel back another layer in a **Discuss and Dialogue** session. As we're soaking in their perspective, we echo their thoughts and concerns, setting the stage for: "I'm really curious about what you like and what bugs you about your social media use. Let's unpack all this". You're in charge of creating a space where they feel heard and understood, clearing the way for an honest exchange about navigating the digital world intentionally.

Spotting a chance to sprinkle in some wisdom, we might roll out an **Up to You Suggestion**. With a laid-back approach we could offer, "Hey, if it sparks your interest, I've stumbled upon some cool ways to keep social media use in check, like setting screen time limits or adjusting your feed to better suit you. Can I share?" If the moment feels right for a gentle nudge, we can **Lean In** if we have any concerns. Maybe you want to suggest they could strike a better balance between their social media habits and the rest of their daily tasks. Maybe you can start with tech-free dinners or set a gadget curfew, and see how it changes things. Suggesting without dictating opens the door for them to take the lead on finding a healthier digital rhythm.

These chats with your young adult aren't exactly a walk in the park. As they grow up, the whole **Lean In** strategy might not hold the same weight. Given that we've never navigated the always-online world during our own coming-of-age, our well of wisdom might seem a bit dry, especially when it comes to learning from our own hits and misses. That's precisely when turning to a **Third Party** or tapping into the expertise of seasoned pros could really make a difference. For solid insights on navigating the digital domain, I recommend "commonsensemedia.org." This group offers a look into the digital content landscape, providing ratings and reviews for the latest in entertainment, along with top-notch guidance for parents. Predicting how future tech will reshape your kid's social world is a tough call, but adapting to cultural and technological shifts is part of every generation's journey. Remember, you did tackle your share of upheavals too. You're more equipped for this than you think.

CHAPTER 6 - FINDING AND ENGAGING WITH YOUR COMMUNITY

When we dive into the five facets of wellbeing, figuring out what exactly community wellbeing means can be a bit of a head-scratcher. At its simplest, it means being actively involved in your community, knowing and supporting the folks around you, and feeling that same support in return. It includes feeling the safety and comfort of your neighborhood and having fun spots to hang out and unwind. While it shares some common ground with social wellbeing, Rath and Harter highlight it separately. They argue that even though having tight-knit relationships is key, for many across the globe, that's just one small part of the bigger picture. The old saying goes, "It takes a village to raise a child," but the truth is, we never outgrow our need for that village. That sense of belonging and collective support, no matter our age, contributes much to our lives.

In an era where we're often watching our screens, making real-life connections is incredibly important. It's more than just feeling like you fit in; it includes embracing the rich tapestry of viewpoints and life stories surrounding you. This journey doesn't just broaden our horizons. It deepens our empathy and develops our understanding of the diverse world we live in. Getting involved in our community can also lead to unexpected leadership opportunities, challenging us to grow in new ways. It plays a crucial role in carving out our sense of purpose, offering a depth that virtual interactions can't easily match.

Beyond making friends, getting involved in our community can also give our physical health a boost—think joining a gardening club or making a habit of nature walks. It's a win for our mental health too, as it chips away at feelings of isolation and loneliness. Adults who are really plugged into their community tend to bounce back faster; they've got this shield against stress and tough times, thanks to the support system they've built through active engagement. So, what's the takeaway for our young adults? It's about encouraging them to find their niche in the community, and discover first hand how connections can fortify them against life's ups and downs

This topic is a biggie, but let's separate it into four pieces. Kicking off, we've got to juggle two flavors of happiness—eudaimonic and hedonic. Yep, it's all Greek to me too, but here's the gist: we're talking about deep, meaningful joy versus quick-hit pleasures. The goal? We're rooting for our young adults to chase after both happiness types, and guess what? Their community is a goldmine for finding both. It's possible to balance those profound, purpose-driven moments with the lighter, laugh-out-loud ones, and let the community vibe boost them in their quest for a well-rounded, happy life.

Let's also explore the art of expanding social circles. It's crucial to ask: Do our young adults have the ability to mingle with new faces and spark fresh connections in their community? Then there's the spiritual angle, whether it's hitting a local meditation center, or joining a church group, many folks, young and old, find a deep sense of community through religious or spiritual practices. It's a big piece of the puzzle that deserves a shout-out, as it often plays a key role in how connected and supported people feel within their wider community.

Hedonic Happiness: Exploring the Spectrum of Happiness From Hedonic Joy to Eudaimonic Fulfillment

First up, let's decode the happiness concept, starting with

"hedonic" happiness—psychology folks also call it "subjective wellbeing". This one has to do with chasing feel-goods of the moment and steering clear of the bummers. When we're talking about feeling a burst of joy in the here and now, that's hedonic happiness in action. It's those sparkly moments of pleasure that pop up from fun stuff we're doing or the cool things happening around us. Essentially, it's happiness that's all about soaking up positive vibes of immediate experiences and external happenings.

On the flip side, "eudaimonic" happiness involves digging deeper. Eudaimonic happiness occurs when we find the feeling where we're living true to ourselves, tapping into our virtues, and hitting our stride with our potential. This kind of joy doesn't just pop up; it's built from the inside out, rooted in personal growth and the milestones we achieve. Think of it as the long-haul kind of contentment that blooms from engaging in activities that really mean something to us. This happens when we learn to embrace who we are, steer our own ship, and evolve along the way. This flavor of happiness, often dubbed "psychological wellbeing" by the experts, is the rich, fulfilling backdrop of a life well-lived, marked by self-acceptance, autonomy, and ongoing personal development.

To truly thrive, we must pursue both types of happiness, and our community is a goldmine for this pursuit. Take, for instance, the pure joy that comes from being part of community festivities—cultural traditions, public gatherings, you name it. Or imagine the buzz from linking up with clubs or groups, whether you're playing on a sports team, geeking out in a hobby group, or swapping thoughts in a book club. These social playgrounds are ripe with chances for light-hearted fun and relaxation. Diving into volunteer work can also pump up our hedonic happiness. In this way, we can enjoy those warm, fuzzy feelings that come from meaningful and enjoyable activities and interactions with like-minded individuals. Across every community in the U.S. there are so many ways to step out, have a blast, and maybe even click with a new friend amidst shared laughter and good times.

The WISE Approach to Enhancing Hedonic Happiness

Applying the **WISE** framework to boosting community wellbeing through hedonic happiness is all about encouraging our young adults to dive into what their community has to offer. They should be eager to explore and discover the activities available around them. This involves being **Willing to Learn** about their community's offerings and setting some solid **Goals** to actively participate in these opportunities. Have they taken the first step to **Initiate and Implement** by joining in on community events or groups that pique their interest? As they navigate through life, it's crucial they keep up the **Sustained Practice**, consistently engaging with their community and fulfilling their commitments. It's important that they're open to **Evaluate and Evolve** their involvement, looking out for new adventures or more fulfilling experiences that could elevate their happiness and satisfaction. It's possible to keep the spark of joy alive by continuously seeking out and embracing the myriad of experiences their community has to offer.

Fostering Community Engagement with the ADULT Method

When we bring the WISE goals into play, we focus on setting clear benchmarks for what we hope our young adults will achieve in their community engagement. Shifting gears to the **ADULT method**, we step into the role of a supportive ally, guiding them through their exploration and involvement in community activities. We kick things off with a simple **Ask**: "Have you discovered any community events or groups lately?" This opens up the opportunity to **Discuss**, where we can dig deeper: "Which activities really excited you, and what was it about those that stood out?" Next, we might offer an **Up to You Suggestion**: "Totally your call, but have you thought about joining the local sports league? Or maybe giving those pottery classes a go?" We're capable of nudging them to consider options they might not have considered themselves. There are times when **Leaning In** feels right: "I've been thinking, joining that book club could be a fantastic way for you to connect with some new faces around here." Whether they're new in town or just looking to expand their social circle, this could be the answer. If they're still figuring out where to start, pointing them towards a **Third Party** might do the trick: "Why not take a look at the local tourism bureau or chamber's website? They might have a rundown of clubs or upcoming festivals that could catch your eye." As a parent, you're capable of empowering them to take the initiative, explore their interests, and weave themselves into the fabric of their community.

The core purpose of the ADULT method is striking a balance between cheering on your young adult's independence and stepping in with support. Guiding them towards discovering and jumping into community activities is a surefire way to boost their hedonic happiness. It's our job to be there to assist without overshadowing their journey, helping them carve their own path to happiness and fulfillment within the community.

Eudaimonic Happiness: Unlocking Eudaimonic Happiness - Lifelong Learning and Community Engagement

Eudaimonic happiness, with its deep roots in meaning, purpose, and long-term fulfillment, aligns closely with what Rath and Harter describe as high community wellbeing. It's the feeling that your life has depth and direction, a crucial ingredient for thriving. Yet, it's often the trickiest concept to fully understand and foster, especially in our kids. That's precisely why it fits so snugly into the community wellbeing chapter of this discussion. The idea that we all need a supportive community—our own "village"—doesn't fade as we grow older; if anything, it becomes more essential, reminding us that no matter our age, the sense of belonging and contributing to something larger than ourselves leads to deep, lasting happiness.

Our advice begins with a big push for pursuing lifelong learning —think workshops, seminars, and local events. This journey of continuous discovery isn't just about stacking up knowledge; it's a pathway to personal growth and building a life that's rich and overflowing with meaning. Young adults can also be nudged towards volunteer work that resonates with their values, giving them a solid sense of contributing to something that matters. Whether they're passionate about green initiatives, social justice, or sprucing up the neighborhood, these experiences are not just about giving back; they serve as a chance to lead, connect, and weave strong ties with folks who get where they're coming from.

At the heart of eudaimonic happiness is this very act of stepping up and pouring energy into our communities. Leading by example is known to inspire this kind of engagement, but even if you're not out there as much as you'd like, it's perfectly fine to champion your young adult's involvement. Their contribution feeds into a bigger picture, strengthening the community fabric, and kicking off a positive feedback loop that's essential for everyone's wellbeing.

The WISE Goals for Community Connection

Diving into community involvement with the **WISE** approach is a game-changer for young adults seeking meaning and fulfillment. It all begins with being **Willing to Learn** and wanting to **Set a Goal**—are they ready to explore the impact community engagement can have on their sense of purpose? Setting goals to actively participate in community life that mirrors their values is the next step. Then, it's about **Initiating and Implementing**, finding activities that resonate with their beliefs. Consistent involvement and **Sustained Practice** cultivate a feeling of belonging and purpose, but remaining flexible is key. As their journey **Evolves**, being open to **Evaluate** and explore new avenues for engagement ensures their community connection remains a vibrant source of personal growth and satisfaction for them.

Leveraging the ADULT Method for Deeper Community Engagement

When applying the **ADULT** method to boost eudaimonic happiness, we kick things off with a straightforward **Ask**: "Have you done something lately that made you feel like you made a difference or fulfilled you in some way?" This question opens the door to **Discussion and Dialogue**, where we might start with: "What did you like about that? Would you want to keep doing it if you had the chance?" If we're aware of a similar opportunity, we might slide in an **Up to You Suggestion**: "This might pique your interest. There's a new event or group popping up in the community. It seems to be about something I know you're passionate about." For those moments when it feels right to be more assertive, we **Lean In**: "You seem to really care about this topic. Helping others who share your passion could be a really cool experience." And, of course, if pointing them towards a **Third Party** or **Trained Expert**' seems like the best route, we're ready to make that recommendation.

Guiding our young adults with the ADULT approach empowers them to engage with community activities that do more than just spark joy—they foster personal development. True community wellbeing goes beyond mere participation; another benefit is finding things that resonate deeply with their individual sense of purpose, ensuring that each interaction and activity enriches their lives and aligns with their broader goals.

Networking for Wellbeing

Cultivating a strong sense of community wellbeing hinges on our ability to connect and engage meaningfully within our local environments. We've explored various activities that can enhance both hedonic and eudaimonic happiness. Now, let's dive into the art of networking—a crucial skill for fostering these connections. Defined simply, networking involves taking proactive steps to form and nurture relationships with others. This skill is indispensable for community involvement across various activities and equally important for career progression. Even in educational settings, where professional development is the focus, networking skills can be taught to young adults, including those who are more introverted. However, mastering networking requires a deep dive into the methodologies and underlying reasons behind it, emphasizing its importance, not just for career advancement, but for enriching community engagement as well.

The motivation to engage with our community often stems from the desire to deepen our sense of belonging and interconnectedness. This engagement is a key ingredient in leading a life that's not only fulfilling, but also well-rounded. It establishes a network of support, offering access to advice, mentorship, and companionship, which proves invaluable during both personal and professional challenges. This connection facilitates personal growth by introducing us to diverse ideas and viewpoints. The variety of individuals we meet beyond our immediate family and friends broadens our horizons, helping us to expand our knowledge and refine our opinions. It's through these external interactions that we can begin to grow and adapt.

Networking within our community might also unlock doors to professional opportunities, from uncovering job openings to garnering valuable career insights. I often remind my students of the power of networking—many career paths are paved through the relationships we build and maintain. Therefore, cultivating a broad network within our community can lead to tangible benefits, especially in the professional realm.

Business coaches often highlight a concept known as "value exchange," which, in a professional setting, refers to the mutual benefits each party can offer. When applied to community networking, this concept transforms into a commitment to enriching the lives of others, not just seeking personal gain.Therefore, the power of networking extends beyond just impressing those in higher positions—it's about connecting with a wide array of individuals, including peers and fellow community volunteers.

Embracing this approach necessitates a belief in our ability to contribute valuable assets, be it our unique skills, knowledge, or simply our time and presence. It involves a journey of exploration to find the perfect alignment between our offerings, our passions, and the needs of the community. While our primary aim isn't self-promotion, active participation in community initiatives can naturally lead to establishing a personal brand. Showcasing our expertise and consistently demonstrating our values and dependability can subtly influence a broad spectrum of future prospects. Though it's not our direct intention, the development of a personal brand can be beneficial to our commitment to community networking and volunteerism. This personal brand isn't crafted with self-interest at heart, but emerges organically as we genuinely contribute to the community, aligning our actions with our core values and the collective good.

In the earlier sections of this chapter, we discussed numerous pathways for fostering community ties, from participating in volunteer activities and supporting local causes, to immersing oneself in community events or workshops, and joining clubs or groups that resonate with our interests. An additional strategy worth considering is the strategic use of social media and online community platforms. Digital tools like "Meetup.com" or local Facebook groups serve as valuable resources for aligning personal interests with available community activities and organizations. For many, initiating connections digitally leads to more comfortable face-to-face interactions, easing the transition into active community involvement.

Embracing community engagement often requires stepping outside our comfort zones, utilizing networking strategies in professional environments. This approach broadens our social horizons and enriches our sense of belonging and contribution to the community fabric.

Navigating Community Connections: Utilizing WISE Goals and ADULT Strategies

Incorporating the **WISE** goals, we want our young adults to be **Willing to Learn** and **Set as a Goal** to have deep, widespread connections with the community they choose to live in. As parents, it's our aspiration to guide them in **Initiating and Implementing** effective strategies that foster their support network and enable them to contribute positively to the lives of others. Achieving **Sustained Practice** in this realm means they are also skillful at **Evaluating and Evolving** their community engagement, finding a harmonious balance between their passions, what they can offer, and the community's real needs and values.

The **ADULT** method starts with **Ask**: "Have you had the chance to connect with people in your new community?" This question sets the stage for **Discussion**, gauging their level of active involvement and connection with their neighbors: "Did you meet anyone at the festival you attended last week?" If it seems like they're hesitating to dive in, we can provide a gentle nudge or **Up to You Suggestion**: "You're free to take or leave this idea, but have you thought about calling back that person you talked about last week?." When the moment calls for a more direct approach, we can **Lean In** with encouragement: "Why not give that guy from your bowling team a call? You've always said you had a lot in commonl." And if they're navigating a new community that they're not familiar with, recommending a **Third-Party** resource could be beneficial: "Have you thought about joining the chamber or the Rotary Club? I know those organizations are designed to help people meet each other."

It is important to acknowledge that reaching out to make new connections can be challenging, and not every attempt may lead to success. The point of this chapter is to convince you that, though the rewards might be intangible, they're significant and worth the effort. Hundreds of thousands of people the world over have agreed that engaging and being connected to your community are important for thriving. By fostering the necessary skills in our young adults, we're directly contributing to their sense of community wellbeing, encouraging them to step out, take risks, and ultimately find their place in their social realm.

An Erick Story: Finding Community
"When my daughter was debating a few years ago whether she should leave her first job after college, we discovered we had accidentally done something right. We'd taught our daughter how to use her community.

Everytime she called to talk about this particular problem she shared how she had just gotten off the phone with another friend. Apparently she was getting and listening to advice from a large group of people who were not her family. They weren't necessarily telling her what to do, but she was obviously taking it all in and valuing every piece of advice she got. That included ours but it certainly didn't stop with ours.

We learned to call this ever-larger group of friends and mentors my daughter's 'board of directors.' She's consulted them quite a lot over the years. It's an informal group and she changes who she talks to based on her needs. Some of them are her age and bring an incredible diversity of skills and life experiences. Others are older and are more like mentors. Those often come from her work or academic worlds. What has always struck me was how much they genuinely care for my daughter. Every single one gives my daughter their very best advice, and even when I completely disagree with what they advise, I know they are always trying to do their best by her. Another thing I've noted: my advice doesn't seem to carry any special weight. But I guess that's OK. I tell myself her life is more like her friend's life than the one I lived at her age anyway.

When I asked her recently about her 'board', she attributed this openness to our modeling. I guess she overheard how my wife and I quite often consulted someone else in our back and forths about a wide range of topics. I hadn't thought about it much when it was occurring but I guess we were good examples of a communicative, open team. I do remember regularly debating decisions in front of our kids. (Though not always. My daughter doesn't know about the many debates we had out of ear shot when it concerned one of them.) We made frequent references to other friends and mentors and our daughter said she didn't find it awkward to hear what other people thought about her dilemmas. However, she always took them with a grain of salt. The decisions were ultimately hers.

My daughter also explained that being a caring, trusted adult in the lives of others is a role she aspires to. She can't wait to be an aunt, through bloodline or otherwise. She loves helping her friends' kids since she doesn't have any kids of her own. I can remember all of the roles she had during and after college where she helped young adults, particularly young women with problems both small and serious. She has always been interested in being a trusted confidant or source of outside knowledge.

I interpret this to mean she both knows how to engage and depend on her community and also how to give back to it - a truly necessary piece for high community wellbeing. We all need a trusted 'board of directors' that includes more than our parents, and we need to serve on many other 'boards of directors' as well. That is how I now conceptualize true community wellbeing. And in retrospect, I *learned this from my daughter. But that's OK. I'm not surprised to learn she's now on of my 'board of directors.' She's got a very smart momma."*

Spirituality and Religion: Valuing the Connection and the Role of Spirituality and Religion in a Thriving Life

The landscape is shifting – fewer folks are filling churches, but many are still finding a spiritual connection. The Pew Research Center sheds light on this trend, noting a dip in regular religious service attendance, yet an uptick in individuals embracing a sense of spiritual peace and universal wonder. It appears that, nationally, there's a pivot towards personal spirituality, even as traditional religious affiliations see a decline. Generations are subtly redefining their spiritual journey, moving away from conventional religious structures towards a more individualized sense of spirituality. It's a nuanced change, where the essence of spirituality is gaining ground, crafting a balance between formality and personal belief.

Contemporary research in psychology and social sciences consistently highlights that a key ingredient to a thriving life is a deep-seated sense of awe and appreciation for our modest spot in the cosmos. This acknowledgment of the universe's vastness and our small part within it fosters a profound sense of wonder and connection. Hence, it's essential not to lose sight of the significance that spirituality or religion might play in our children's lives. I aim to share some thoughts on the importance and the "how" of nurturing this path. It's not just about adhering to traditional practices, but finding personal resonance in the grand scheme of things, be it through spirituality or religion. This journey is pivotal, offering grounding, perspective, and a greater sense of purpose, all crucial elements in cultivating a life rich with meaning and fulfillment.

The avenues through which young adults can engage with religion or spirituality are likely more diverse than many realize. The immediate thought might be the traditional route of attending regular religious services. Beyond that, they might consider the array of special events, social gatherings, and communal celebrations that various religious institutions—like churches, synagogues, mosques, and others—regularly host. It's possible they have fond memories of such experiences from childhood, even as they now navigate a phase of questioning and reevaluating their faith, both publicly and privately. This period of exploration is a natural part of their journey, offering them a chance to discover a spiritual or religious path that resonates with their evolving beliefs and values.

But religious and spiritual organizations frequently offer more than just traditional services; they provide a variety of study groups and workshops that cater to the interests of the youth. Young adults have the opportunity to participate in discussion groups focused on ethics or explore different spiritual practices. What's often understated is how these gatherings are a conduit for forging close-knit relationships with individuals who resonate with similar beliefs and values.

Such settings have historically been, and likely will continue to be, pivotal spaces where both adults and young adults find significant segments of their community. These religious and spiritual engagements offer more than just faith-based activities; they provide a sense of belonging and connection. Speaking from personal experience, I've found a substantial part of my community within these spiritual practices, underscoring their value in fostering meaningful, shared connections.

Bridging Faiths and Fostering Leadership: Nurturing Young Adults in the Digital Spiritual

Era

Many spiritual events are designed to transcend the boundaries of individual faith traditions, offering enriching opportunities for interfaith dialogues. These platforms are instrumental in fostering connections that extend beyond one's own religious background, allowing participants to discover and appreciate shared values across diverse spiritual landscapes. Engaging in such dialogues can be an eye-opening experience, particularly for young adults, offering them a broader perspective on faith and spirituality.

Additionally, these gatherings often provide young adults with the chance to step into leadership roles. Such experiences are invaluable, contributing significantly to their personal growth and sense of fulfillment. Being in a position to lead or facilitate discussions can enhance confidence and deepen engagement with their spirituality, but also the spirituality of others. Seeing spirituality from the perspectives of others plays a crucial role in their own spiritual development and overall sense of thriving.

In the contemporary digital landscape, the significance of connecting with religious and spiritual communities through online platforms cannot be overstated. Social media and online forums have become instrumental in maintaining connections and staying informed about spiritual events and gatherings. Many religious institutions are investing in their online presence, creating vibrant communities and virtual services that resonate with the modern congregant. For young adults, these digital spaces might offer a more comfortable starting point or serve as a bridge to more traditional, in-person engagements.

The importance of these diverse opportunities lies in the communal aspect of religious and spiritual practices. Engaging with these communities brings individuals into contact with others who share fundamental values, fostering a fertile ground for deep, meaningful relationships. Such environments provide a substantial support network for emotional and sometimes material assistance.

Envisioning a thriving individual includes seeing them at peace with their purpose and their understanding of the cosmos. Whether it's through traditional religious observance or a more personal spiritual journey, exploring connectedness and purpose is vital. Encouraging young adults to explore and embrace these aspects of life, be it in a church or through a screen, can be pivotal for a well-rounded, fulfilled, and grounded individual.

Integrating WISE Goals and ADULT Methods in Spiritual Exploration

The **WISE** goals framework encourages young adults to embark on a spiritual journey, starting with a **Willingness to Learn** and **Setting a Goal** to dive into the realms of spirituality and religious thought. This initial step is crucial for them to begin to understand and appreciate the universe's mysteries and their place within it. Through **Initiate and Implement**, they can explore various spiritual practices or religious philosophies, gradually building a personal connection to these profound concepts. The aim is for them to achieve **Sustained Practice**, where the serenity and depth that come from a spiritually enriched life become a consistent part of their existence, nurturing inner peace and broadening their worldview. Finally, we'd like to see the **Evaluation and Evolution** of their thinking.

The **ADULT** method complements this by starting with an **Ask**, prompting the young adult to reflect on their current perspectives on religion and spirituality. This opens up a space for **Discussion and Dialogue**, where there's an opportunity to exchange views or simply provide a supportive platform for them to articulate their evolving beliefs. An **Up to You**

Suggestion might follow, introducing them to spiritual groups, events, or resources that align with their burgeoning interests, yet leaving the choice firmly in their hands. There are moments to **Lean In**, where encouragement to engage more deeply with spiritual communities might be appropriate, especially if it seems to resonate with their search for meaning. Introducing a **Third Party**, like community or campus organizations such as the Fellowship for Christian Athletes, offers a supportive environment for young adults to explore spirituality within a group setting. Such organizations can play a pivotal role, especially during transitional life phases like college, providing a sense of belonging and a network of like-minded individuals.

Each family's approach to this journey will be unique, influenced by their values, traditions, and the individual's personal inclinations. Encouraging young adults to explore, question, and develop their sense of spirituality and religion is not just for their personal growth, it also helps them construct a framework for meaning and purpose that will support them throughout their lives. While the aim isn't to sermonize on religion and spirituality, it's essential to acknowledge how significant the role is they play in shaping a young adult's community wellbeing. These elements, often deeply interwoven into the fabric of community life, can be pivotal in experiencing belonging, purpose, and connectedness. And discussing religion and spirituality is crucial toward understanding the myriad ways through which individuals can experience and contribute to the collective wellness of their communities.

A Riley Story: Finding My Own Way Religiously

"Growing up, I went to church with my father and siblings every Sunday. I also attended Sunday school all throughout my childhood. This was a practice we all expected, and were all used to. But as a younger child, I didn't always enjoy going. We grew up Catholic, and it was very difficult for me to understand. Up until quite recently, I struggled to feel a connection with my church.

When my siblings and I turned 16, we were allowed to start making decisions about our own faith. My parents wanted us to be able to practice our faith however we wanted. As a busy high schooler, I unfortunately removed myself from the church entirely. I was very active and involved in a lot of activities, and oftentimes, could not fit going to church in my schedule. We would still go to church on holidays, but besides that, I had very little involvement for several years.

My brother attended a Lutheran youth group throughout highschool and into college, and this is where he found his home. He became thoroughly involved, and started working as the youth director at his church. As a family, we wanted to support him, so we began to attend services at his church. This is where my passion for my faith was reignited. I realized through a smaller Lutheran church, that you can have a close community. My perspective entirely changed.

When I went to college I decided I would start to attend my university's Fellowship of Christian Athletes (FCA) group. Making this decision has truly bettered my life. As I mentioned, community is very important to me. The community at FCA was so welcoming and warm, and I was able to find a group of other athletes that had good relationships with their faith. I have been able to get closer with these new best friends in a whole new way. I am so grateful my parents allowed me to make my own decisions when it came to my faith. If I continued to go to service at my old church, I am not sure my faith would be where it is today. Having the opportunity to choose where I am most comfortable has changed my life for the better."

CHAPTER 7 - FINDING A CAREER YOU LOVE AND VALUE

Embarking on a career that is both personally fulfilling and beneficial to the community poses a significant challenge. Rath and Harter's research illuminates the profound impact of career satisfaction on overall wellbeing, suggesting that thriving in one's professional life is a key determinant of personal happiness. This subject boasts more than a little complexity. We'll distill our insights into four comprehensive categories to provide a structured approach to this vast topic.

The initial focus will be on the pivotal phase of choosing a career. While parents undoubtedly influence this decision, it's crucial that the young adult has the autonomy to make this choice for themselves. The anxiety many students experience around pinpointing the "right" career is substantial, and this decision-making process will be the core of our first category. We'll explore strategies to ease this stress and ensure that the chosen path aligns with their interests, values, and the impact they wish to make in the world.

Subsequently, we'll look into how positive psychology can be integrated into professional life, enhancing job satisfaction and career fulfillment. This second section will draw from real college-level course material about happiness in the workplace. We'll emphasize how understanding motivations and recognizing strengths and weaknesses can profoundly influence our career trajectory and daily job satisfaction.

The journey through professional life involves the choices we make, as well as how we respond to challenges and relationships that come our way. In the third segment of this focus, we'll introduce and examine the concepts of grit and growth mindset—key attributes that can prepare young adults for the inevitable ups and downs of work life. Understanding how to persevere through setbacks and develop resilience can significantly influence how they navigate their career paths and overcome the obstacles they will undoubtedly face.

We will also focus on the intricacies of workplace relationships. The dynamics of interacting with colleagues, superiors, and subordinates can greatly impact one's job satisfaction and career progression. We'll explore strategies for fostering positive, productive relationships in a professional setting, emphasizing communication, empathy, and mutual respect.

Choosing a Meaningful Career

Navigating the career selection process involves crucial early steps, one of which is encouraging your child to consider a wide array of career possibilities, not just those seen within the family. While it's common for young adults to gravitate towards professions familiar to them because of their parents or relatives, it's essential that this isn't the sole guidepost. Comfort from familiarity is understandable, but the objective should be to have them explore and consider a broad spectrum of opportunities, ensuring they make a well-informed choice based on a comprehensive understanding of the possibilities out there.

Another vital aspect to consider is aligning their career choices with their personal strengths and interests. Often, the initial career decision is made in the teenage years, a period when many young adults are still in the process of discovering who they are and what they excel at. Keep in mind that the part of the brain that affects decision-making and self-awareness, the prefrontal cortex, doesn't fully mature until the mid-20s. Because of this, it's not at all unusual or unreasonable for preferences and career paths to evolve. This developmental phase highlights the parent's role in guiding the young adult to recognize their strengths and potential, aiding them in making informed decisions about their early career choices, but making sure they don't feel pressured to lock themselves into any decision permanently.

It's also worth noting how common career shifts are as individuals more closely examine their professional lives. I often advise my college students not to fixate on finding the "perfect" career, but to focus on gaining entry into the workforce and starting their professional journey. The future is inherently unpredictable, and the notion of a linear career path is increasingly outdated. Embrace the concept that initial jobs are stepping stones, offering professional connections, valuable experiences, and insights that will shape their understanding of what they want from a career.

This perspective can be comforting not only to young adults embarking on their career journey, but also to parents guiding them. It's entirely normal for someone to pivot to entirely different roles or industries as they grow and learn about themselves. Encourage your child to be open to change. It takes much of the pressure off if they view their early career choices as part of a larger, evolving journey, rather than a fixed destination. This approach can lead to fulfilling and surprising opportunities, ensuring they find satisfaction and joy in their professional life, even if there are unexpected turns along the way.

It's essential to weigh the available career options and gauge the feasibility of achieving those goals given their current circumstances. Once a career path is selected, the focus shifts to detailed planning and the practicality of its execution. Consider the timeline: How many years might it take to reach the desired point? Various careers demand distinct commitments, from extensive higher education to the resilience and hands-on dedication required in fields that offer the deep satisfaction of collaborative efforts or tangible creations.

Another piece of advice we should emphasize is the value of experiential learning through internships, part-time jobs, or volunteer work. Such experiences are invaluable, providing real-world insights, honing practical skills, and enhancing employability. Additionally, finding mentors is crucial. Connecting with experienced professionals who can share wisdom, guidance, and industry insights can profoundly impact one's career trajectory.

Remember, the journey to a fulfilling career is seldom linear and often involves exploring diverse avenues before settling on a path that resonates both professionally and personally. The route to career satisfaction can be winding, requiring adaptability, perseverance, and an openness to learning from each experience along the way.

Navigating Career Development with the WISE Framework

Tackling career development with the **WISE** strategy is a bit of a juggling act, considering how unpredictable and varied a career journey can be. Young adults should aim to be open-minded and proactive— **Willing to Learn** about a vast spectrum of career opportunities and setting clear, achievable goals. This strategy helps ensure they're on track to hit milestones without unnecessary backtracking, especially when redoing steps might come at a price.

For the **Initiate and Implement** part, it's key for them to dive into research, meticulously planning the necessary actions to reach their career aims and start weaving their network with industry folks and mentors who can offer golden nuggets of advice.

Sustained Practice isn't just sticking to the plan—it's about consistently beefing up both their technical chops and those all-important soft skills, like how to communicate well, play nicely with others, and tackle problems head-on.

When it comes to **Evaluate and Evolve**, they get to tweak their game plan as needed, staying nimble and responsive to feedback. This stage should help ensure that they're always moving in the right direction with their career goals.

Seeing them master this cycle—ready to adapt, keen to grow, and equipped to navigate the twists and turns of their career — signals that they're well-prepared to take on the professional world and are guiding themselves towards a fulfilling and successful future.

Navigating Career Choices with the ADULT Method

Starting with the **Ask** phase, we initiate the conversation gently, sparking curiosity rather than dictating directions. "What catches your interest when you think about future careers? Is there a particular path that feels exciting to you?" This nudges them to ponder their aspirations and share their visions.

Moving to **Discussion and Dialogue**, we dive deeper, exploring their thoughts and feelings about potential careers. It's an opportunity to reflect together: "What skills do you feel you need to develop for this path? Are there aspects of this career that you're still curious about?" This stage is crucial for uncovering insights and understanding their perspective more clearly.

Transitioning to an **Up to You Suggestion**, the emphasis is on empowering them. The approach is non-imposing: "It's entirely your choice, but if you're open to it, I'd love to share some thoughts. Maybe there's a course or a workshop that could give you a taste of what this career involves?"

If it seems appropriate to **Lean In**, we can gently steer them towards actionable steps, ensuring they feel supported yet autonomous: "You've shown such a keen interest in [specific interest]. What about exploring opportunities where you try this out? It might give you valuable insights into whether it's the right fit." Or, you could look for **Third Party** advice from a guidance counselor or advisor.

Employing the **ADULT** method in this manner creates a supportive backdrop for young adults, enabling them to navigate their career path confidently. It strikes a balance between offering guidance and allowing them the space to make their own informed decisions, ensuring they feel empowered to carve out their own future.

A Riley Story: Priorities Matter In Big Decisions

"Entering your college years and deciding what you want your major to be and where you want to go can be very intimidating for a sixteen year old. I certainly know it was for me. To make things even more of a toss up, I was being recruited by multiple different schools for both field hockey and lacrosse. At the time, I was so stuck and so anxious when it came to making a decision. So many 'what-ifs' circled through my brain. What if I'm not happy at the school I choose? What if I don't like my major? What if playing a sport doesn't end up working out? And a seemingly endless barrage of more doubts.

When it came to picking a school, my parents were incredibly clear with me about one thing. 'No matter what and where you choose to go, pick a school that you would be happy at even if you no longer played a sport. Put your education first, athletics second.'

At the time I was skeptical about this because I was SURE I would spend my four years playing a sport. I could already picture myself walking across the stage to receive my diploma with a sash that read 'student athlete.'

But eventually, those dreams came to a crash. Sophomore year I finally decided I was not happy playing field hockey any longer. I struggled with many extenuating circumstances, and for the sake of my mental health and well-being, decided to step away. So did many other players on my team who were going through the same things I did. Some were/are my best friends. It was a hard decision.

But now, I could not be happier. I am incredibly pleased with my classes, as well as my outside involvement. My parents' advice truly saved me when it came to making a decision about where I wanted to go to school. Whether it's sports, clubs, greek life, or maybe even the food choices on campus (trust me, it matters), there will be factors that make an impact in where you decide to pursue your degree. The bottom line is, it is most important to push the academic side, because that sets the foundation for your career and impacts your preparation for success in the real world."

Motivation and Happiness at Work: Exploring Career Self-Actualization Through Maslow's Lens

Understanding what it means to truly enjoy work is crucial in guiding young adults toward a fulfilling career. It's about creating a path that's not only financially rewarding but also personally meaningful and engaging. Given the unpredictable nature of the future job market, our focus should shift from specific job skills to broader aspects such as attitude, perspective, and approach to work. These elements are instrumental in shaping a young adult's career satisfaction and sense of purpose, regardless of the evolving employment landscape.

Supporting young adults in this journey involves fostering a mindset geared towards adaptability, resilience, and meaningful engagement in their work. Encouraging them to stay open to learning, to embrace change, and to find value in their contributions can make a significant difference in how they perceive and experience their career. We want to help them develop a positive framing of work, one that sees beyond the paycheck to the broader impact of their professional lives. By instilling these values, we can assist them in building a career that not only supports their livelihood but also contributes to their overall sense of wellbeing and fulfillment.

Initiating our exploration, let's revisit a foundational concept you might be familiar with—Maslow's Hierarchy of Needs. Abraham Maslow presented a theory several decades ago, suggesting that our pursuit of higher-level aspirations hinges on the fulfillment of more fundamental needs. These layers range from basic physiological needs to the pinnacle of self-actualization, where an individual focuses on realizing their potential and engaging in fulfilling, purposeful work. The aspiration for young adults is to navigate their careers from this top perspective, harnessing their unique talents to make a meaningful impact.

Self-actualization is essentially about finding that sweet spot where personal strengths and job responsibilities align perfectly, facilitating a state of "flow." This concept, popularized in psychology, refers to those moments when we are so engrossed in a task that time and self-awareness seem to vanish. It's an experience of being fully immersed and engaged, often leading to peak productivity and satisfaction. Observing a young adult deeply absorbed in a task, like playing a video game, offers a glimpse into what achieving flow in a career might look like.

Our goal in nurturing young adults' career paths is to help them reach this stage where work isn't just about earning a living but about contributing to their fulfillment and self-realization. Encouraging them to seek roles that ignite their passion and align with their strengths is key to them experiencing flow and, subsequently, achieving a state of self-actualization in their professional lives. This alignment not only benefits their sense of personal accomplishment but also enhances their overall wellbeing and satisfaction with their career choices.

Of course, encouraging self-care is crucial in guiding our young adults towards a fulfilling career. By nurturing their overall wellbeing across life's various domains, they can better concentrate on achieving career satisfaction and potentially reaching self-actualization. A key aspect of this is advocating for a healthy work-life balance, ensuring they understand the importance of preventing burnout and effectively managing stress.

It's also essential for young adults to recognize and celebrate their successes, whether they're monumental achievements or small victories, and to remain open to continuous learning and the unpredictable journey their career paths may take. Instilling a positive work mindset can significantly contribute to their career trajectory, helping them view their professional experiences not just as obligations but as opportunities for growth and enjoyment.

Demonstrating a healthy attitude toward work ourselves can powerfully convey this perspective, showcasing that work can indeed be rewarding and enjoyable. By role modeling such positivity, we can profoundly influence our young adults' approach to their careers, encouraging them to find joy and purpose in their professional endeavors.

WISE and ADULT Application

Utilizing the **WISE** framework can guide our young adults to be proactive in aligning their careers with their personal strengths and interests. The aim is for them to be **Willing to Learn** about how their personal attributes fit within the workplace and to **Set Goals** that align their career path with their intrinsic skills and passions. As they **Initiate and Implement** this approach, they actively engage in shaping their career based on self-awareness and strategic planning.

This journey of self-discovery and career alignment is ongoing, demanding **Sustained Practice**. Over time, this leads to the **Evaluation and Evolution** of their career choices, ensuring they are moving toward roles that fulfill them, rather than away from dissatisfaction. The goal is for them to proactively seek opportunities that resonate with their capabilities and aspirations.

When applying the **ADULT** method, we start by **Asking** open-ended questions about how they find their work's meaningfulness and satisfaction. The **Discussion** that follows should delve deeper, looking beyond immediate complaints to understand their core experiences and feelings about their work.

An **Up to You Suggestion** can be made when it's time to consider whether their current role aligns with their values and skills or if a new direction might be more fulfilling. This suggestion respects their independence, offering them a chance to reflect and decide without pressure.

As they mature, the need to **Lean In** should diminish, but we must be ready to offer guidance when necessary, especially in pivotal career moments. And sometimes, suggesting a **Third Party or Trained Expert** might be the best course of action, providing them with additional perspectives or specialized advice to navigate their career path effectively.

Through these strategies, we can support our young adults in developing a career that not only provides for them but also grants a sense of accomplishment, purpose, and personal growth. Engaging in career discussions with young adults, especially those in their 20s, can indeed be a nuanced task. While it's essential to have these conversations, the approach should be more of a collaborative exploration rather than a directive one. Parents, often understanding their children profoundly, play a crucial role, yet the dynamic must be balanced. Embracing the role of a co-explorer allows for an open, supportive dialogue where insights are shared, and guidance is subtly woven into the conversation, maintaining respect for the young adult's autonomy and individual journey. This approach acknowledges the complexity and personal nature of career choices, aiming to empower rather than dictate.

Having Grit and Resilience: Facing Setbacks

In this section, we'll address the inevitable challenges of the workplace with a blend of realism and optimism. Previously, we've explored selecting fulfilling careers and fostering job satisfaction. Now, we're shifting focus to the less-than-ideal days. Every career has its highs and lows, and it's crucial for our young adults to be equipped with the right tools to navigate these moments.

We'll discuss strategies for maintaining confidence and resilience, even when the going gets tough. This isn't about sugarcoating the realities of work life but rather acknowledging that bumps in the road are normal and manageable. It's about empowering our young adults to face obstacles with determination, a constructive mindset, and a touch of grace. They'll learn how to approach difficult situations not just with grit but with a perspective that transforms challenges into opportunities for growth and learning. Let's prepare them to handle work's ups and downs with resilience and a balanced, positive outlook.

The key to navigating the professional landscape, especially for young adults, is recognizing that setbacks are often veiled opportunities for growth rather than signs of defeat. In the early stages of any career, when experience is limited, encountering challenges is inevitable. Young adults are particularly prone to facing hurdles early in their careers as they refine their skills and explore their capabilities.

Our role as parents is crucial in guiding them to view these challenges through a lens of learning rather than failure. It's about striking the right balance—helping them discern when to persevere and when it's genuinely time to pivot. Our support can fortify their resilience, encouraging them to see that growth and learning are continuous journeys.

We should aim to inspire our young adults to view every challenge as a chance to evolve. Encouraging them to reflect on their experiences critically—not to dwell on the setbacks but to extract lessons and insights—is vital. This mindset shift from viewing failure as a stop sign to seeing it as a stepping stone can profoundly impact their career resilience and overall satisfaction.

Exploring the realms of grit and resilience offers a refreshing perspective on navigating life's ups and downs. Grit is about embracing the long haul, sticking to your long-term goals with spirit, while resilience is your comeback power, bouncing back from challenges with grace and vigor. Studies echo that these traits are the unsung heroes behind the scenes of success, emphasizing that steadfastness and adaptability are key players in the journey toward achievement.

Encouraging our young adults to lean into discomfort and view feedback as golden nuggets of growth is essential. These qualities aren't just spontaneously generated; they're honed through life's trials and triumphs. By engaging with their passions and challenges robustly, young adults can begin to incorporate these traits into their character fabric.

The notion of a "growth mindset", championed by psychologist Carol Dweck, complements this beautifully. It's a liberating belief that our abilities aren't set in stone but are sculptable with persistence and effort. It's about seeing the path to mastery as a dynamic journey, where challenges are milestones of progress, not roadblocks. Encouraging a growth mindset in our young adults transforms their approach to life's hurdles. It nurtures a culture of continuous learning and adaptability, setting the stage for a lifetime of exploration, resilience, and ultimately, a fulfilling and successful journey.

Confronting imposter syndrome is also essential, especially for young adults stepping boldly into their careers. This syndrome manifests as persistent self-doubt, a sneaking suspicion of being a fraud, despite evident successes. It's a widespread phenomenon, yet often cloaked in silence, with many individuals wrestling privately with their apprehensions, hesitant to share their fears.

As more seasoned individuals, we've come to recognize that such feelings of insecurity are a universal aspect of the human condition, common across various stages of life and career. Acknowledging and normalizing these insecurities can significantly bolster our young adults. Offering assurance and understanding, we can help them grasp that experiencing doubts and insecurities is a natural part of the growth journey, not a sign of inadequacy or lack of merit. Our support is pivotal in helping them combat imposter syndrome, reinforcing that these internal misgivings do not undermine their achievements or their capabilities. Sharing our own experiences and struggles with self-doubt can light the path forward, showing that these feelings are neither defining nor limiting. Instead, they reflect the natural uncertainties that accompany personal development and expansion into new roles or challenges.

Fostering open conversations about these internal challenges empowers young adults to recognize and overcome imposter syndrome, validating their successes and encouraging a healthy self-perception. It's about reinforcing their belief in their own worth and their ongoing journey of self-discovery and growth, ensuring they feel grounded in their achievements and confident in their potential to evolve.

Applying the WISE and ADULT Strategies

Incorporating the **WISE** goals into nurturing grit, resilience, and a growth mindset begins with fostering a **Willingness to Learn**. Young adults should be encouraged to explore and understand their responses to workplace challenges, aiming to **Set a Goal** that commits to cultivating a positive, resilient attitude towards their career. **Initiating and Implementing** involve actively applying strategies that reinforce a constructive outlook, embracing failures as learning opportunities, and persevering through adversities. **Sustained Practice** is about continuous engagement with this process, learning from each experience, and adapting strategies accordingly. The hallmark of their progress is their ability to **Evaluate and Evolve** their approaches, transforming workplace challenges into opportunities for growth, and diminishing feelings of imposter syndrome.

The **ADULT** method helps along this journey, starting with **Asking** insightful questions that dive into their emotional and mental landscape concerning work. This opens up a **Discussion and Dialogue** that should be empathetic yet probing, aiming to uncover underlying feelings and perspectives on their challenges. An **Up to You Suggestion** might involve proposing they consider new strategies or perspectives, emphasizing that change is within their control. There may be moments to **Lean In**, offering direct guidance or an alternative viewpoint based on your broader life and career experience. Yet, it's vital to balance this with their independence, ensuring they feel empowered to make their own decisions. In some instances, suggesting a **Third Party or Trained Expert** could be invaluable, particularly if both of you are stuck on how to resolve a difficult situation.

Ultimately, using the **WISE** and **ADULT** frameworks, parents can guide their young adults toward embracing their career journey with confidence, armed with the tools to develop resilience, maintain a growth mindset, and navigate the inevitable challenges with grit and grace. This approach aims not just for career success but for the cultivation of a fulfilling and adaptive professional life.

Navigating Work Relationships: Understanding Workplace Dynamics

Navigating workplace relationships is pivotal for young adults as they lay the foundation for their career journey. Early career experiences can often help young adults understand if they are motivated more by the tasks at hand or the relationships they cultivate. Those who are "task-oriented" derive immense satisfaction from the work itself, relishing the challenges, problem-solving, and the sense of accomplishment from completing projects. Their motivation is fueled by the mastery of tasks and the intrinsic rewards that come with it.

Conversely, individuals who are "relationship-oriented" find joy in the social dynamics of the workplace. They thrive on teamwork, enjoy collaborating on projects, and value the interpersonal connections made with colleagues. They find fulfillment in the camaraderie and collaborative spirit of working in teams.

Understanding whether one is driven more by tasks or

relationships is key to finding job satisfaction. It's not about one being better than the other; rather, it's about recognizing where one's sense of engagement and fulfillment stems from. Some individuals might discover that they require a balance of both to feel wholly invested in their work.

Diving into the workplace is like stepping onto a seesaw, where balancing task-focused drive with the knack for nurturing work relationships is key. Young adults should get the hang of this balance, recognizing that while some colleagues might be all about the business, others are there for the camaraderie as much as the paycheck. One can think of it as deciphering a social code —figuring out if someone is more of a doer or a schmoozer, or maybe a bit of both, and then using that insight to click with everyone from the taskmaster to the team cheerleader.

However, polishing up on professionalism is always going to be important —showing up on time, dressing the part, and minding office etiquette. It's the universal backstage pass to fitting in smoothly and making those work relationships count.

It's also important to remember the core traits of teamwork, where harmonizing diverse opinions and mastering the art of feedback exchange play starring roles. Many of our young adults will need to find their voice to articulate personal limits clearly and confidently, ensuring they stand firm when situations threaten their comfort zone. This skill is essential not just for their wellbeing but for fostering a respectful work environment where everyone understands where lines are drawn.

Yet, even with the best-laid boundaries, disagreements are part and parcel of any job. The trick lies in tackling these clashes with a blend of professionalism and tact, ensuring they're nipped in the bud before they bloom into full-blown issues. Our young adults need to learn how to strike that delicate balance between standing their ground and keeping the office peace, transforming potential workplace turbulence into learning curves.

Navigating this sometimes requires a sense of empathy and insight, looking into the why behind a colleague's challenging behavior. Understanding doesn't mean excusing, but it can pave the way for more harmonious interactions. And when things veer into the territory of harassment or bullying, it's about knowing when and how to escalate matters to higher-ups, be it a manager or HR, ensuring safety and respect aren't just office buzzwords but lived realities.

Learning the art of boundary-setting is a crucial chapter in the professional growth story of every young adult. They have to find their voice to articulate personal limits clearly and confidently, ensuring they stand firm when situations threaten their comfort zone. This skill is essential not just for their wellbeing but for fostering a respectful work environment where everyone understands where lines are drawn.

Entering the workforce also brings a pivotal lesson not often covered in textbooks: the art of managing up. This skill is crucial for young adults to grasp as it involves understanding how to subtly influence and effectively collaborate with those above them in the workplace hierarchy. They will have to align their work ethic, initiatives, and outputs with the expectations and priorities of their boss, thereby positioning themselves as indispensable assets to the team.

Effective communication plays a key role here. They will have to maintain a transparent channel with the boss, sharing updates on progress and hurdles effectively, ensuring there are no surprises that might catch the boss off guard. This requires a delicate balance of providing just the right amount of information — enough to stay on the radar without overwhelming with details.

Ultimately, managing up is about embracing a broader vision of the organization, understanding the strategic priorities from a leadership viewpoint, and molding one's contributions to resonate with those overarching goals. It transforms young professionals from passive participants to proactive, strategic contributors in their career journey.

The leap from the informal student life to the structured professional world can be stark. Ideally, they'll find a mentor in their boss who will guide them through the nuances of workplace etiquette. However, they might need to navigate this new terrain with some autonomy, adapting to the unique culture of each workplace. This learning curve is particularly significant for those who draw energy from interpersonal connections.

Navigating Work Relationships: Integrating WISE and ADULT Strategies

The application of the **WISE** goals offers a structured pathway for young adults to enhance their understanding and management of workplace relationships. The starting point involves being **Willing to Learn** the nuances of work interactions and the impact they have on job satisfaction. They should embrace the concept that people derive fulfillment from work differently, whether through task completion or enriching social interactions. **Setting the Goal** to master the art of professionalism is pivotal, recognizing that it lays the foundation for respect and smooth interactions in the professional realm.

The **Initiate and Implement** stage is where they actively engage with their work environment, factoring in their inclination towards tasks or relationships. This step is about translating awareness into action, whether it's finding joy in collaborative efforts or ensuring tasks are aligned with personal and organizational objectives. This phase is crucial for honing skills in teamwork, feedback exchange, and the expression of professional needs and boundaries.

As they move into **Sustained Practice**, they must refine their skills in assertiveness, emotional intelligence, and effective conflict resolution. This continuous improvement is vital for adapting to diverse workplace scenarios and enhancing overall job satisfaction. The **Evaluate and Evolve** phase requires them to reassess and adjust their approach to workplace relationships, aiming for a harmonious alignment with their career goals and team dynamics.

Implementing the **ADULT** method starts with an **Ask**, prompting them to reflect on work relationships and their balance between task-oriented and relationship-oriented satisfaction. The subsequent **Discussion and Dialogue** encourages them to think about the intricacies of workplace interactions, exploring motivations and value alignments. An **Up to You Suggestion** could offer gentle guidance towards proactive solutions, while the option to **Lean In** allows you to emphasize the importance of strategic communication with colleagues and superiors.

Sometimes, the introduction of a **Third Party or Trained Expert** becomes essential, providing external insights or mentorship to navigate complex professional landscapes. These mentors or career coaches can offer tailored advice, aiding in your young adult's journey towards adeptly managing workplace relationships.

Emphasizing the significance of positive workplace connections, and equipping young adults with the tools to foster these relationships, is a transformative aspect of their career development. Through consistent practice, adaptability, and strategic learning, they can evolve into independent professionals capable of thriving in any work environment, fully embodying the autonomy and resilience we hope for them.

An Erick Story: They'll Have To Navigate A**holes Just Like You Do

"Our oldest was switching jobs after spending about two years and an internship at the company that had gotten him excited about his career. He was sad to leave. He liked the people and, from what he had told us, most people there liked him. Well, most of them.

He was moving to a new city and rejoining some of his highschool and college buddies. There was also a substantial raise involved. It all seemed to be going well except for one supervisor he had at his current company. This guy apparently took it personally that our son was moving on and decided to come after our son with a vengeance. This all came out slowly over the course of several weeks, but apparently this 50-something-year-old went to my son's current bosses and bad mouthed him terribly. He became incredibly rude, abused his position of power, and threatened to call my son's new company and bad mouth him. Months later he did call my son's new company and ask that my son be taken off of a project.

During our phone calls we tried to calm our son down. We had him get reassurances from his other superiors that they didn't feel the same way and that they thought this one guy was being a real a**hole. But apparently no one could stop him. I think at one point he had been told to back off, but I don't think it worked.

My son was rightfully worried about what his new company was going to think of him. We counseled him best we could, that they would see through this guy and realize he was just being an a** hole, but there was nothing either we or him could do about it. It was going to be one of those things he had to just live through. We promised him it was all going to be better someday. It was a tense few weeks.

But to my son's credit he showed up to work every day, finished out his month, and moved to the new city. Things went well at this new job and a few months in he told me the guy had left the old company and moved on to somewhere else. Apparently no one missed him.

Everything worked out at my son's new job but we still remind him *that sometimes, you just have to live through the bad times that a**holes create. If you've tried to do every reasonable thing you can about it, then try to relax and focus on the good people. The bad people eventually get what's coming. Society really doesn't like a**holes."*

CHAPTER 8 - FINANCIAL WELLBEING ISN'T ALL ABOUT MONEY

Emphasizing financial wellbeing, it's essential to recognize that life satisfaction isn't about the size of our bank accounts. Surpassing friends or neighbors in earnings doesn't equate to happiness. Instead, the essence of financial contentment lies in stability—having sufficient income to live without constant anxiety about finances. This sense of security, free from the strain of choosing between essential expenses like housing or food, is what truly contributes to our overall sense of wellbeing and thriving, as highlighted by Rath, Harter, and other researchers. It's not wealth, but the absence of financial stress, that helps to lay a more stable foundation for a fulfilling life.

Researchers have discovered many different types of personal relationship with money, often revealing patterns that transcend mere spending, saving, or investing habits. These patterns, or "money scripts," as identified by experts like Brad and Ted Klontz, are ingrained beliefs about money that we often adopt unconsciously. These scripts, categorized into four types, shape our financial behaviors and decisions. They are often rooted in our upbringing and the financial atmosphere of our childhood homes. Recognizing these scripts is crucial, as they play a significant role in our financial wellbeing and the money-managing choices we make. As parents, it's vital to understand and reflect on these money scripts, ensuring that the financial examples we set help support the development of healthy financial attitudes and practices for our children.

The "Money Status" script represents a mindset where an individual's self-esteem is tightly intertwined with their financial status. People with this script view their net worth as a direct reflection of their self-worth, often pursuing wealth as a means to secure or enhance their social standing. They tend to associate financial success with personal happiness and might overspend to showcase their affluence, prioritizing outward appearances of wealth over genuine financial stability. This approach can lead to risky financial behaviors, including accumulating debt and living beyond one's means, ironically risking the very financial security and social status they seek to uphold. Recognizing and addressing this script is crucial to fostering a healthier relationship with money, one that values financial wellbeing and genuine contentment over superficial symbols of success.

The "Money Worship" script encapsulates the belief that happiness and fulfillment are directly proportional to one's financial wealth. Individuals who subscribe to this script are convinced that an increase in income or possessions is a straightforward path to a happier life, epitomized by the notion that "more money equals more happiness." This belief system can propel individuals into a relentless pursuit of wealth, often at the expense of personal wellbeing, leading to potential workaholism, accumulating debt, and chronic financial dissatisfaction. The critical misunderstanding here lies in the expectation that financial gains alone can fulfill all emotional and psychological needs, overlooking the multifaceted nature of personal contentment. This skewed perception can result in a neglect of other vital aspects of life, creating a paradox where the quest for financial abundance could hinder genuine experiences of thriving and wellbeing. Recognizing and recalibrating this script is essential for fostering a more balanced and fulfilling relationship with money, one that acknowledges wealth as a tool rather than an end goal.

The "Money Avoidance" script is characterized by a deep-seated ambivalence or outright negativity towards money, often stemming from past adverse experiences or ingrained beliefs. Individuals with this mindset tend to shun financial matters, possibly due to a sense of unease, guilt, or a belief that money is inherently corrupt or problematic. This script can manifest in various ways, from neglecting personal finance management to self-sabotaging financial success, driven by an underlying discomfort with the idea of wealth accumulation. Such individuals may also exhibit a pattern of giving money away excessively, driven by guilt or a desire to disassociate from the perceived burdens of wealth. This approach, however, can lead to financial instability and prevent the achievement of a secure, thriving state. Addressing this script involves fostering a healthier relationship with money, recognizing it as a neutral tool that can support personal goals and wellbeing, rather than a source of anxiety or moral conflict.

The "Money Vigilance" script is characterized by a consistent wariness or anxiety regarding financial matters, regardless of the actual amount of money saved or accumulated. Individuals who embody this script often engage in prudent financial behaviors, such as regular saving and practicing frugality. While these habits can contribute to a solid financial foundation, they may also lead to undue stress about financial security and the future. Such individuals might find it challenging to make expenditures, even when they are reasonable or necessary, due to a deep-seated fear of financial instability. Although this cautious approach can safeguard against imprudent financial decisions, it may prevent individuals from fully enjoying the peace of mind and comfort that financial stability is meant to provide. Striking a balance between careful financial management and the ability to relish the rewards of one's diligence is crucial for those guided by the money vigilance script, ensuring that their financial diligence enhances their overall sense of wellbeing and life satisfaction, rather than detracting from it.

Finally, the concept of a balanced "Goldilocks" money script, though not explicitly identified by researchers, represents an ideal approach to financial management. This hypothetical script combines a sensible level of the "money vigilance" mindset with moderated elements of the other three scripts, ensuring a well-rounded financial perspective. Individuals embodying this script understand the importance of living within their means, thereby steadily accumulating wealth. However, they also maintain a flexibility that allows them to enjoy life's pleasures and experiences that money affords, avoiding the pitfall of excessive frugality that tends to diminish life's enjoyment.

This balanced approach is crucial because money scripts are often ingrained in individuals from an early age, heavily influenced by the attitudes modeled by their parents. Both behaviors around money—like giving allowances or enforcing savings—and the more subtle cues given through discussions about finances, can determine a child's financial beliefs and behaviors. So, for parents, self-awareness is key. Recognizing and understanding one's own money scripts can help in intentionally guiding children towards a healthier, more balanced relationship with money. By exhibiting a thoughtful approach to finances, parents can instill in their children the values of financial responsibility, the joy of financial freedom, and the importance of aligning financial decisions with personal values and goals.

Learning to Budget: Strategies and Managing Money

The third/third/third budgeting approach is a straightforward, yet effective, financial planning tool to help young adults begin to manage their finances. The concept is simple. As soon as a young adult begins earning, while still living at home, have them divide their post-tax income into three equal parts. One-third goes to the parents for covering essential expenses, such as bills like cell phones and car insurance. Another third is for savings, promoting financial security and responsibility. The final third is designated for discretionary spending, allowing for personal enjoyment and learning the value of a dollar. This budgeting method is not just a theory, but a practical strategy that works successfully for many. It instills a balanced financial discipline, encouraging young adults to allocate their income wisely, while still enjoying the fruits of their labor. Adopting this method early on can set a solid foundation for financial wellbeing, teaching the importance of balancing necessities, future financial health, and current enjoyment. It's a formula that promotes and ensures that young adults learn to manage their money effectively, paving the way for a stable and prosperous financial future.

Budgeting isn't just about numbers; it's a strategic way to map out financial life. For young adults, mastering the art of budgeting means more than just jotting down numbers. They should actively engage with their finances, keeping a close eye on both incoming funds and outgoing expenses. This active engagement helps them stay attuned to their financial realities, enabling them to make informed choices and adjust their habits as needed.

In today's tech-savvy world, there's no shortage of tools to help with this task. Apps and spreadsheets can simplify tracking, turning what once might have been a tedious chore into a straightforward, even enlightening, activity. The real crux of budgeting lies in setting a plan and sticking to it, tracking every transaction to ensure it aligns with planned expenditures and savings goals. Encouraging young adults to embrace this method means empowering them to take charge of their financial wellbeing, steering clear of unnecessary debt, and paving the way for a secure financial future. Whether they're tech enthusiasts, or prefer the simplicity of pen and paper, the essential factor is consistency in monitoring their budget, ensuring they're always on track with their plans.

Another important point to remember is to encourage your young adult to distinguish between needs and wants. This is crucial for fostering long-term financial wellbeing. It's vital they learn to prioritize their spending, steering clear of unnecessary expenses and impulsive buys. The third/third/third budgeting approach can be a practical tool here, as it sharply illustrates the value of each dollar—when only a third of their income is available for discretionary spending, each purchase decision gains weight, encouraging more thoughtful and deliberate spending.

Instilling the practice of budgeting and money management as a routine part of life is essential. For young adults, this habit should become so ingrained that it's second nature, performed almost subconsciously. It's beneficial to introduce the concept that saving for significant future expenses is not just prudent, but also rewarding. Whether it's setting aside funds for a vehicle, educational expenses, or a special item like a gaming system, the discipline of saving teaches the value of delayed gratification. As they mature, the practice evolves to encompass long-term goals, contributing to a sense of security and peace of mind. This foundational habit is what leads to the wellbeing described by Rath and Harter, highlighting the importance of financial stability in overall life satisfaction.

Integrating WISE Goals into Financial Habits

Adopting the **WISE** approach to budgeting and financial management means guiding our young adults to be proactive with their finances. They start by being **Willing to Learn** the ins and outs of budgeting, setting clear **Goals** to manage their money wisely. The **Initiation and Implementation** phase is crucial—they actively apply their budgeting plan, adjusting to live within their means while prioritizing expenses, savings, and discretionary spending. This habit evolves into a **Sustained**

Practice, adapting as their financial situation changes, ensuring they're always in control of their finances. The ongoing process involves **Evaluating** their habits and **Evolving** their strategies to optimize savings and spending as their income grows. This disciplined approach to budgeting is a lifelong skill that will yield continuous benefits.

Applying the ADULT Method toward Financial Literacy

Incorporating the **ADULT** method into our young adults' financial education begins with an **Ask**—initiating a conversation to gauge their understanding and current practice of budgeting. This leads to a **Discussion and Dialogue**, providing insights into their financial awareness and their position relative to the **WISE** goals. Depending on their developmental stage, our intervention should be measured; it's crucial to assess whether they are at the right point considering their age and life experience.

An **Up to You Suggestion** is made with tact, offering advice or alternatives without pressure, ensuring they understand it's their choice to embrace or disregard the advice. When necessary, we might **Lean In**, offering specific resources or tools to simplify budgeting or help overcome any obstacles they might face.

If progress seems stalled, or if they're struggling with the concept, introducing a **Third Party or Trained Expert** could be beneficial. Websites like NerdWallet can provide them with accessible, user-friendly financial education, empowering them to make informed decisions and changes in their financial habits. This approach ensures they're equipped with knowledge and resources to manage their finances effectively, fostering independence and long-term financial wellbeing.

An Erick Story: Budgeting Is Easy If You've Been Doing It All Along

"I don't know where my wife got the brilliant idea that our kids should put their money into three buckets the minute they started making their own money, but it worked. She had an unbreakable rule from the very first kid and his very first job: one third of your take-home pay goes to us for various expenses like your phone, gas money, car insurance, etc... One third had to be put in savings, which we periodically checked on. The last third you could spend on yourself. A wrinkle that I didn't even appreciate until years later is that she also made them write her a check for their bill-payment one third. That meant they had to open a bank account and get checks. We also made them get a debit card that was tied to their bank account so it wouldn't work if they ran out of money. We didn't let them carry credit card balances as teenagers.

What we wanted them to learn was to pay your bills first. Bills were non-negotiable and had to go out of the account first. Second was savings. What was left was your spending money. Ironically, the third child gave us the most grief about this arrangement. But we stuck to it and I even overheard his older brother tell him once, 'Dude, you're going to like this later. I have spending money in college because I can dip into my savings account now.'

We also had each get the parent-child Discover card so they had an emergency credit card (that we could monitor). This allowed them to build up a credit score under our supervision.

Now, more than 10 years later, each has a savings account, a monthly budget, and they spend within their means. None of them have a big credit card balance. Each has their spending patterns. One's bought a house, one travels constantly, and one is into fancier cars. But by all accounts they are managing their money well.

Training your child to budget early on is definitely the way to go. You can have a lasting impact on their financial wellbeing. It just takes a few 'rules' that they get used to. It's easy to budget if you've been doing it all along."

Dealing with Credit and Debit: They are Not Bad Words

Understanding credit and debt is crucial for young adults, especially in an era where financial obligations like credit card debt, car loans, and student loans are escalating rapidly. Post-pandemic, while some Americans managed to reduce their credit card debts with the aid of stimulus checks, more recently the trend has reversed with debts climbing once again. Given the soaring costs of college education, which have consistently outpaced inflation for years, it's essential for young adults to grasp the significance of credit and debt management as foundational elements of sound financial planning. This knowledge will empower them to make informed decisions, ensuring they can navigate the complexities of personal finance with confidence and foresight.

Initiating a conversation about credit literacy is a pivotal step in educating young adults about financial responsibility. Understanding the intricacies of a credit score, including its calculation based on payment history, credit history length, new credit, and outstanding debts, is key. It's crucial for young adults to recognize the impact their credit behavior will have on future financial opportunities, such as obtaining loans or leasing apartments. I had a standout student once who couldn't rent an apartment when she left for graduate school due to a lack of credit history. This illustrates the unintended consequences of avoiding credit entirely. Therefore, it's advisable for young adults to initiate their credit journey responsibly, ensuring they have a history of timely payments and managed credit lines, which contributes positively to their credit score. Regular monitoring of credit reports is also vital, enabling them to identify any inaccuracies and maintain a healthy credit status, thus safeguarding their financial future.

Instilling the habit of timely bill payments in young adults is a cornerstone for maintaining a healthy credit score. It's crucial for them to comprehend the ripple effects of punctuality in bill payments, including the avoidance of late fees and the potential enhancement of their credit rating. This practice preserves their financial health and influences the interest rates they might be offered on future loans for significant purchases like cars or homes. Encouraging the setup of reminders or automated payments can be a game-changer, ensuring they consistently meet their financial obligations and reducing their stress.

Furthermore, it's vital for young adults to grasp the comprehensive costs associated with borrowing. Understanding concepts such as the Annual Percentage Rate (APR) and how interest accumulates over time is non negotiable for making informed financial decisions. By recognizing how to scrutinize and potentially negotiate better interest rates, and the benefits of exceeding minimum payment amounts, they can significantly mitigate the long-term expenses of loans. This knowledge aids in reducing the overall debt burden and also empowers them to manage their finances more effectively.

Grasping the distinction between productive and detrimental debts is also important for young adults. Productive debts can be seen as investments in one's future; they include commitments like mortgages, where the monthly payments contribute to homeownership rather than simply covering rent. Similarly, student loans can be considered beneficial if they lead to increased earning potential, outweighing the initial cost of education and interest payments over time. Conversely, detrimental debts are those that diminish financial stability and value. High-interest debts from credit cards are a prime example, where the interest payments can quickly snowball and exceed the original borrowed amount, offering no long-term financial return or growth. It's important for young adults to discern which debts can be leveraged for future gain and which could lead to financial setbacks. Understanding this difference empowers them to make informed decisions about borrowing, ensuring that their debt contributes positively to their financial trajectory, rather than impeding it.

When young adults encounter debt, they should learn how to approach it with a strategy, utilizing resources that often suggest paying down high-interest debts, while keeping up with minimum payments elsewhere. Advising them to tread cautiously with new debt is crucial. They need to understand how debt payments can contribute to financial stress and the lost opportunities for saving or investing. But it's also beneficial to set realistic expectations about starting modestly, emphasizing that their first home or car will likely not match the comfort or status of what they grew up with. This gradual approach allows for financial growth and prevents the common pitfall of becoming "house poor" or "car poor". This is where disproportionate amounts of income are funneled into mortgages or car payments, leaving little for savings, emergencies, or leisure. Instilling a gradual wealth accumulation mindset helps young adults prioritize financial stability and long-term goals over immediate gratification.

Embarking on the path to a debt-free life before hitting retirement might seem like a lofty target for young adults, yet it's profoundly shaped by the financial habits they cultivate early on. This quest for financial independence isn't just about dreaming big—it demands the creation of concrete debt reduction strategies, coupled with a commitment to adhere to these plans consistently over the years. As parents, our role transforms into one of a cheerleader, celebrating their financial victories and persistently motivating them to remain on course. Encouraging this mindset from the get-go can highlight the substantial impact of their initial financial choices, guiding them towards a future unburdened by debt, where financial stability and peace of mind are achievable.

Mastering Financial Health: The WISE and ADULT Approaches

Applying the **WISE** goals means our young adults are **Willing to Learn** about credit literacy, smart debt strategies, and the freedom they will ultimately achieve living a debt free lifestyle.

We want them to **Initiate and Implement** appropriate short-, medium- and long-range plans to accomplish their financial goals. As older adults we know it will take **Sustained Practice** and continual learning about changes in the credit and debt marketplace. This means we'll want them to be able to **Evaluate and Evolve** their credit and debt strategies.

When we use the **ADULT** method we'll begin with an **Ask**. "How confident are you in your long range plan to achieve financial health? Do you believe you know enough about credit and debt to avoid paying fees or the inflated true cost of borrowed money?" In the **Dialogue and Discussion**, depending upon their age, we'll want to make sure they know a great deal about the topics I've listed above. Maybe we'll occasionally offer an **Up to You Suggestion** about further learning opportunities, or perhaps choices they hadn't considered. There might be times when we **Lean In** and argue for or against a choice we've heard them discuss. As they get older, we'll have to respect their autonomy and maybe watch them make a few mistakes. However, in the long run, sometimes a mistake early on can have tremendous benefits later for how they handle credit and debt. Since very few of us are certified financial planners, we'll very likely use a **Third Party or Trained Expert** in this particular category. It might even be the case that we should go along with them on that learning journey, since many of us still have a lot to learn about credit and debt.

Teaching Early How to Save and Invest

Mastering the art of saving and investing is pivotal for young adults. Instilling the habit of early saving can set the stage for a financially secure future, largely due to the magic of compound interest. This phenomenon allows the value of savings to grow exponentially over time, even at modest interest rates. Resources like Suze Orman's books or NerdWallet offer great insights into leveraging this power effectively. Starting to save from a young age, even during the teenage years, can lead to significant wealth accumulation in the later stages of life. I've always encouraged my children to prioritize their retirement savings to ensure that, by their 50s, they're free from the stress of not knowing if they can ever retire.

It's crucial for young adults to grasp the basics of investing, beyond the foundational practice of saving. Understanding how to maximize benefits, like ensuring they contribute enough to their retirement accounts to get their company's match, is just the starting point. They should also become familiar with various investment vehicles, including stocks, bonds, mutual funds, and particularly, the nuances of target date funds and the differences between pre-tax and post-tax investment options. Knowledge about Roth IRAs, 401(k)s, and 403(b)s is essential. While it's not necessary to master all these concepts immediately, it's important that they don't delay too long in their earning years without exploring the diverse investment opportunities available to them. Encouraging a proactive approach to learning about these options can set them on a path to informed investing and long-term financial growth.

Understanding risk management is also an essential part of financial literacy for young adults. They need to assess their comfort level with various investment risks and comprehend the fundamental balance between risk and potential reward. Typically, higher potential returns come with increased risk. Adopting a strategy similar to target-date funds—taking on more risk earlier in one's career and transitioning to lower-risk investments as they approach retirement—can be wise. However, it's crucial to clarify that personal comfort with risk varies and should guide investment choices. Diversification also stands out as a critical concept in managing investment risk. It involves spreading investments across various asset classes to minimize the impact of poor performance in any single area. Young adults should learn the importance of diversifying their portfolio to safeguard against market volatility and align their investments with their evolving risk tolerance. Strategic asset allocation is key, allowing individuals to adjust their investment approach in response to changing market conditions and personal financial goals. While these are foundational strategies, it's essential to consult with a certified financial planner for tailored advice, especially for those who are not well-versed in these areas themselves.

In addition, they might someday need to do all of this in concert with a potential life mate. I read once that most arguments in marriages occur over finances. You'll want to stress to your young adult that they'll need open lines of communication about financial goals, expectations, and money habits with their partner. They'll need to engage in joint planning, budgeting, saving, and investing. The better they can align their financial goals, the easier achieving financial health will be. These need to be ongoing conversations that allow the couple to adapt to new goals and life changes.

Applying the WISE Goals and ADULT Method

Embracing financial literacy is a vital aspect of modern life, particularly in the intricate landscape of American finance. The **WISE** framework offers a structured approach to this learning journey. Initially, it's essential for young adults to be **Willing to Learn** about the basics of saving, investing, and the importance of setting varied financial goals that span from immediate needs to long-term aspirations. The next step is to **Initiate and Implement**, where they actively start to put their financial knowledge into practice, developing a plan that encompasses savings and investment strategies tailored to their personal goals. The habit of saving consistently forms a **Sustained Practice**, where the focus is on building financial resilience and stability through regular, disciplined actions. Over time, as they gain more experience and confidence in their financial decisions, young adults will naturally **Evaluate and Evolve** their strategies, adapting to new financial insights, market conditions, and personal life changes, ensuring their financial plan remains aligned with their evolving life goals and the financial landscape.

Embarking on the path to financial wisdom with our young adults involves an application of the **ADULT** method, ensuring that our guidance complements their growing independence. As always, we begin with an **Ask**, sparking conversations that respect their growing independence in financial decision-making.

Engaging in **Discussion and Dialogue** provides a platform to share experiences, insights, and maybe a few cautionary tales from our own journeys, aiming to enlighten, rather than direct. Introducing **Up to You Suggestions** allows us to present new financial perspectives or options they might not have explored, gently broadening their financial IQ without imposing decisions.

The **Lean In** phase is crucial but should be balanced; initially, it may involve more direct guidance on effective financial strategies, but as they mature, the emphasis shifts to supporting their autonomous decision-making. Finally, recognizing our limits in financial expertise, and encouraging our young adults to consult **Third Parties or Trained Experts** becomes pivotal, connecting them with professionals who can provide tailored advice and strategies for their unique financial landscapes. This step empowers them to navigate their financial future confidently and even more independently.

Whatever our own financial situation in life, most likely all of us want our kid's situation to be better. The surest way for them to achieve financial health is to save and invest.

Knowing How to Financially Plan: The Need for Expert Guidance

While exploring financial planning and goal setting, it becomes evident that navigating the complex financial world often requires expert advice. The financial landscape is filled with a vast array of investment opportunities, retirement plans, and intricate insurance policies, making it challenging for an individual to navigate without professional insight. Incorporating the "Third Party or Trained Expert" step from the ADULT method is crucial. Seeking a financial advisor isn't just beneficial, it is also strategic. These experts provide personalized, objective advice tailored to your unique financial circumstances, encompassing your risk tolerance and personal aspirations. Encouraging your young adult to engage in regular financial check-ins is also crucial. These routine assessments help them stay aligned with their goals and adapt to any significant life changes, ensuring their financial plans remain relevant and effective.

One strategy is to highlight the benefit of breaking down their overarching financial strategy into smaller, manageable steps. This approach can simplify the financial journey and boost motivation through the achievement of small victories and tangible progress. While it's understood that financial strategies will more than likely evolve over time, possessing a flexible, yet well-defined plan is indispensable for long-term success. Instilling the value of adaptability in financial planning ensures your young adult can navigate the shifting intricacies of personal finance with confidence. This should remain true, especially as their plan changes as they progress through different stages of their career.

SMART Framework for Financial Clarity

Introducing your young adult to the SMART framework can significantly enhance their approach to setting financial goals. This method encapsulates five key principles: Specific, Measurable, Achievable, Relevant, and Time-bound. Each element of the SMART acronym guides the goal-setter to formulate objectives that are clear, trackable, realistic, aligned with personal ambitions, and subject to a definitive timeline.

Although the concept of SMART goals is widely discussed and easy to find information on, it's a fundamental strategy worth exploring together. While you might not have all the tools to help your young adult craft an intricate financial plan — perhaps you're navigating your own financial planning challenges — you can still play a crucial role in motivating them to establish and pursue a coherent financial strategy. Encouraging the adoption of SMART goals aids in immediate financial decision-making and fosters long-term financial independence, which is a key milestone in raising a self-sufficient adult.

Financial Planning with the WISE and ADULT Approaches

It's crucial for our young adults to be **Willing to Learn** about financial planning, setting clear short, medium, and long-term financial goals. As they step into the **Implementation** phase, our role transitions to that of a supporter, celebrating their financial milestones, while respecting their growing independence, especially as they progress through their 20s and 30s. Consistently applying their financial plan, or **Sustained Practice**, is key to transforming strategic financial planning into a second nature, ensuring they can adapt their strategies to align with personal growth and external economic changes. Ultimately, we want them to be proficient in **Evaluating and Evolving** their financial plans, ready to modify their approach in response to life's inevitable shifts.

Initiating conversations with an **Ask** can open up discussions about their current understanding and approach to financial planning. The **Dialogue** that follows allows us to gauge their comprehension and enthusiasm towards financial independence. There's a chance they might be more informed than us due to the vast resources available today. However, if there are gaps in their knowledge, we can introduce **Up to You Suggestions** offering insights while emphasizing their autonomy in decision-making. In their younger years, our influence might be more pronounced, guiding them towards the importance of a robust financial plan. As they mature, we might transition to a more hands-off approach, occasionally **Leaning In**, but mostly taking comfort in their ability to manage their finances independently. Given the intricacies of financial planning, seeking assistance from a **Third Party or Trained Expert** is often a wise step, providing them (and perhaps us) with the expertise needed to craft a comprehensive, long-lasting financial strategy that fosters financial wellbeing and independence.

Echoing insights from Rath, Harter, and numerous scholars, I'd like to emphasize that financial contentment transcends mere accumulation of wealth. Once basic financial stability is attained, mere increases in wealth seldom correlate with heightened happiness. It's also important to note that attaining a state of financial wellness is seldom serendipitous; it necessitates deliberate planning and strategic foresight. It's about striking an equilibrium where financial resources are enough to live comfortably, without the perpetual pursuit of more money tipping the scales of personal joy and contentment. This underscores the importance of proactive financial management to reach a place of security, where financial resources serve life's joys, rather than dictate them.

A Haley Story: You Can Nag Too Much

"In our early college years, I used to give my best friend nonstop grief about her money and spending habits. Abbey, is that another new dress? Did you really need an eighth swimsuit top from American Eagle in the same color? When was the last time you put anything into your savings account? Didn't you say you wanted to buy a car after college? You ate out so many times this week. You know expenses like that add up so fast.'

Was it my place to put in my two cents? Probably not. But I cared about her, so I thought I was doing what was best for her. Oftentimes, as I've also seen with many parents and their children, the more I nagged her, the more resistant and sneaky she got. We've probably all heard that kids of strict parents become the best liars. She started hiding, being secretive about where she went to eat. She started shopping online so I had no ammunition to criticize her with. She shoved new clothes into the furthest corner of her closet. She gradually started wearing her new jewelry with old jewelry, hoping I wouldn't notice. She now acknowledges she was doing these and other things to avoid my criticisms. We've spoken about it a lot now that we've graduated college.

My point is that oftentimes letting kids make their own financial mistakes - within reason - can be more beneficial than bugging them incessantly about their bad spending habits. If they haven't learned about credit and are racking up debt, that's a different story and they could certainly benefit from some intervention and education, but not every situation is going to lead to the end of the world. Sometimes they just have to learn through little mistakes and come to those realizations on their own.

If I stop to think about it, my best friend was certainly becoming more focused on hiding her retail therapy habit from me than she was on actually resolving her spending habit. At the time I'm not sure she even noticed the effects it was having on her savings or the effect it would have on her future self. My nagging was just motivation to put her energy into hiding her spending. I once came home from a class early to find her bent over in our apartment kitchen, stuffing a receipt into our trash can, fast food bag in-hand. When she darted a surprised, guilty glance over her shoulder, I clicked my tongue in disapproval. She blushed, realizing she'd been caught red handed and turned, mouth already open with an excuse on the tip of her tongue. I shrugged at her with a grin, and shook my head as I walked away without interjecting. I was starting to realize that my criticism just wasn't helping. I realized I was distracting her from the problem at hand and pushing her toward other bad habits. I was making her feel like she had to lie about money.

When I finally made an effort to stop bugging her about it, she eventually realized that she did have future goals: important, exciting goals that would cost her serious money. She wanted to go to grad school. She wanted to buy a new-ish Jeep. She wanted to travel to Europe with her boyfriend. These were big goals she'd have to work for and big expenses she'd really have to save for.

Gradually her relationship to money and spending started to change for the better. We're now a couple of more years down the road and she has a 'big girl job' in Philadelphia. She bought herself a Jeep a year ago and is completely in love with it. She's taking care of her credit score by paying her graduate school loans on time, every time. She recently bought plane tickets to France and Switzerland. And what's more? She's doing it responsibly, despite having to figure it all out (pretty much) on her own. I don't think her parents provided the instruction she needed earlier in life on how to handle money, but I'm glad to see her catching on now.

I think if you find your child struggling with a poor spending habit, using the WISE ADULT method outlined in this book will help. Everyone should learn to budget. It's not really that hard. Particularly if you start young. But also remember: sometimes non-stop nagging hurts more than it helps. You wouldn't want your child to learn to hide their spending from you."

EPILOGUE

My wife and I learned many years ago that the "happy times" are the simple, uneventful days that occur between crises. Because there will always be crises when you have kids. And by that I mean simply important phone calls or problems that need solving. All three of our kids called just this week to have long conversations about problems at work or in their relationships. They are currently 30, 29 and 27. Parenting doesn't really ever end.

But we certainly do less "problem solving" than we did when they were younger. Almost all of these phone calls were those first three types of conversations I outlined in Chapter 3: listening to them share their successes, listening with empathy, or just talking. They're grown and independent now and we only offer advice when they ask for it.

But where does that leave you? You may be at the beginning of this long journey. Maybe your kids are still in elementary school? If so, you may certainly use that old stand by "because I said so." The backing off comes as they get older. To do so correctly means you'll be watching their behavior to determine when they should be making decisions on their own. You'll want to hear them think out loud so you find out how they're prioritizing things. Are they ready to make this particular decision on their own? You'll constantly be asking yourself that question.

I confess, I didn't know Riley, Haley and I would write a 48,000+ word book when we started this journey, but it's been a blast. Both have provided invaluable writing advice, but more importantly, they've shared their stories with me and validated my overarching purpose - to help parents raise healthy, independent, thriving adults - as I know they both are.

If you've found this content inspiring, please reach out to me and let me know what you think. Tell me if we've missed something important, or if you disagree with something we've written. All three of us are extremely grateful you've decided to share so much of your time with us. We know you'll enjoy your time as a parent and feel very proud one day of the thriving, young adult you've helped raise. Because, as I've said many times already: parenting is the toughest job you'll ever love. Enjoy the ride!

Made in the USA
Middletown, DE
28 August 2024